# Embrace
## THE LESSONS

# Embrace
## THE LESSONS

Vickie H. Shannon

**BALBOA.**
PRESS
A DIVISION OF HAY HOUSE

Balboa Press books may be ordered through booksellers or by contacting:

Balboa Press
A Division of Hay House
1663 Liberty Drive
Bloomington, IN 47403
www.balboapress.com
1-(877) 407-4847

ISBN: 978-1-4525-3300-1 (sc)
ISBN: 978-1-4525-3302-5 (hc)
ISBN: 978-1-4525-3301-8 (e)

Library of Congress Control Number: 2011903302

Printed in the United States of America

Balboa Press rev. date: 3/14/2011

This book is dedicated to the Universal Intentions that helped create it.

"Be the change you want to see in the world." –Mahatma Gandhi

# CONTENTS

# PREFACE

This book was not intended to be about me. It is a memoir, yet, I truly do not consider myself so significant that anyone would want to read my memoirs. I write to teach. I tell these stories about my experiences in the hope that others will benefit. Much of this book was written over the course of three decades. I've wrestled with what I was trying to convey, what to include, what to take out, and how much to divulge about myself. It is a time marker, consisting of significant events throughout my life that have been memorable because of the lessons learned. If not for the belief that I am here as a student, in this University called Earth, with the ultimate goal of evolving spiritually, then life in and of itself would be an existential purgatory. I'm not much for rhetoric. My writing style has a Dragnet approach ("Just the Facts") that may be described as easy to read in that it is straightforward. I speak my truth, for that is all that I have. My life has been one of nonconformity, not so much because I want to be a rebel, but simply because I am not like most people. That has been my experience throughout life. As a child this disturbed me because it was a constant source of humiliation. Children can be very cruel, and I was frequently cast aside by my peers.

I used to wonder why God made me different from others. It made this journey called life so very challenging because I started out feeling confused, inadequate, and unworthy. Adolescence is difficult enough, and when you become aware of the fact that you are mentally ill, an alcoholic, a lesbian, psychic, and androgynous (long before the term androgynous became en vogue), it is especially challenging to be self-accepting. I decided a long time ago that in order to thrive I would have to find a way to be true to myself. I'm just different. Those that know me love and accept me for who I am. I cannot pretend that I am something that I am not; even if that means that

I am ostracized or shunned. Over the course of time I have become self-accepting and consequently self-empowered. Because the painful elements of my journey have required stamina, I have been blessed with the spiritual growth and development that I otherwise would not have known. This is why it is not uncommon for others to remark: "You are an old soul." Truth be told, I am weathered from the many and varied storms of life.

The original title of this book was Gifts From My Teachers: Stories of Transcendence. I originally chose that title because I wanted to honor the many and varied teachers that have taught me throughout the years. The lessons, however painful, are gifts. I am a willing student and a slow learner. Some of the lessons had to be repeated because yours truly was either too stubborn or ignorant to get it the first time around. Life is cyclic, and what I did not absorb the first time I was able to take notice of the second time. I am comforted by the fact that Life will continue to provide me with the lessons that I need, even if that means reruns and repeats. I no longer see this as failure, but as God's patience with me. The teachers that I speak of are not the traditional teachers that one would find in a school or university. Those teachers I should probably acknowledge separately, for there were many who made a tremendous impact on my life.

The teachers contained within this book were of human, animal, and spirit form that provided an experience for me that was insightful and/or life changing. I may be different, but I'm not special, in that we all have experiences that can be magnanimous in the impact it has on our growth and development. I think many humans operate in a sort of vacuum that lacks depth. It has become so easy to get caught up in the daily living tasks and negative energy patterns of our times (terrorism, global warming, politics, and violence). Depth requires a mindful consciousness. It requires a willingness to be aware, to learn, to grow, to strive toward a personal spiritual evolution. If enough of us do this (and there already is a higher level of consciousness that has been growing in numbers and vibratory energy) then we shall have a spiritual revolution. This is what is necessary to become a global community and save our beautiful planet. I started on this path to save myself. As I age I become more conscious and able to be a small part of a greater whole. I have been blessed by my Teachers. I welcome them into my world, my existence, simply because it makes me a better me.

My Teachers connect me to an Eternal Source that is full of wisdom and love. I share with you my stories of Transcendence, in the hopes that you will become open to your own. The paradox is that we are alone in this journey called life, yet we are never truly alone. We are all connected. There is no separation between you and me. There is no separation between the heavens and earth. I invite you to awaken to your Teachers. Listen, watch, and observe the many forms in which they appear. Open your mind and your heart in order to embrace the lessons.

# ACKNOWLEDGMENTS

To the many and varied teachers that have mentored me throughout the years. I am indebted, humbled, and grateful for their wisdom.

I would be remiss if I did not acknowledge those who encouraged me to write, including my Spirit Guides (Hanna and Tron), Marti Bergeron, the Reverend Dawn Casseday, Sandra Thames, and my mother (Eleanor Simon) and sister (Suellyn Simon). I would also like to express gratitude toward Katrin Hoffmann and Beth Walsh Eriksen for their support and encouragement once I made the commitment to self-publish.

Special thanks go towards Carol Peachee and Laura Hohnecker, two women whose tireless, unconditional, skillful efforts forged a path of hope and gave me the gift of life. Without them, I would not have survived to share my stories. It is through them that I came to Trust the Process and experience Life as worth living. Yes, it *is* worth it. There will always be a Light in my heart for both of them.

*Part 1:*

# GIFTS FROM THE HUMAN EXPERIENCE

# CHAPTER ONE

# THE GIFT OF PAIN

The human condition requires that we experience and incorporate pain into a higher level of consciousness that ultimately serves to transcend one's spirit. As part of the human condition we question why we should feel pain. Indeed, our brains are neurologically set up for pleasure. As a human species we have a low tolerance for pain, which has motivated us to generate things that have made life much less painful. One might even say that we have evolved to the point that pain seems unnatural to us, and has indeed become unacceptable to us. We live in a time of immediate gratification. The invention of the microwave oven was perhaps an important time marker of this new era. Until the microwave came along, we had to spend hours preparing and cooking meals. There was no such thing as a Drive-Thru or Fast Food. It is not uncommon in today's world to wait impatiently for the microwave to "hurry up" and heat up our food. It is also not uncommon to not 'have time' to 'run though a drive thru.'

The invention of the remote control brought immediacy to our finger tips. Some of us remember that children used to serve as both TV antenna and remote control. Remember when your father would say: "Hey, get up and turn the channel. Wait. Stand right there, the reception is better-- and hold your arm--yeah that's good." Back then we had three TV stations— ABC, CBS, and NBC. We thought we hit it Big Time when PBS came upon the scene. Now there are hundreds of channels and we frequently "can't find" anything that interests us. We "surf" the TV, radio, and the web in an attempt to find something that suits our every whim. We live in a time and place where we expect to receive pleasurable/stimulating things almost upon the moment that we desire them. Pain has become unnecessary and unacceptable. Pain has become something to avoid. In fact if we encounter pain, we automatically assume that something is terribly wrong.

We have this unrealistic expectation that we can and should be able to sustain an indefinite period of bliss. In the rooms of 12 Step Programs it is not uncommon to hear people say that they are happy, joyous, and free. Another common expression is that members are "happiest beyond their wildest expectations." Now, I'm not against people feeling happy. In fact, I rejoice in such a blessing. The problem is when people begin to think something is wrong if they are not happy all the time. I like to ground people in the reality that "Happy, Joyous, and Free" is not a place. It is not a destination. It is a temporary emotional state of well-being that is afforded to us as a respite from the daily trek called Life. We cannot be happy all the time. That is just not natural. Even though we have evolved into the Information Age, this does not mean that we are no longer part of nature. There are just some things that we cannot bypass, and one of those is that life is challenging. If you are sad, anxious, upset, hurt, or angry it doesn't mean that something is wrong, it just means that something is. It is as it is. Be with whatever it is, and it too shall pass. Everything comes and goes. That is natural—eternal bliss is not natural.

Pain comes in many forms. There is physical pain, emotional pain, and mental pain. I separate emotional and mental pain because the two feel distinct to me. Emotional pain is a feeling response to an event. Mental pain is typically the result of repetitive beliefs that in turn produce emotional pain (such as sadness or anxiety). As human beings we encounter physical, emotional, and mental pain as part of the experience that life offers. It is through the challenges of physical, mental and emotional pain that we are offered the opportunity for spiritual growth. Spiritual growth is not currently a high priority in this country because it lacks immediacy and requires stamina and a humble approach to pain. Why should I feel pain if

I can take something or do something to bypass such pain? How can there possibly be value in working through pain? The value comes in the lesson learned—be it gratitude, fortitude, self-empowerment, compassion, love.

I believe that we each have our own traumas and challenges in life. The amount, frequency, and depth of these traumas will vary from person to person. For some it may be one major traumatic event in life. For others it may seem to be a never ending cascade of mini traumas. There are those, too, who believe that we chart our traumas and our lessons before we get here (are born). This makes sense to me, as it would be characteristic of a loving God to allow us to participate in our Course of Education. After all, it is all for Glory, all in the name of Love. Of course, I don't feel very loving when I am in the middle of one of my Lesson Plans. In fact, I'm more likely to curse, hold my breath, and stomp my feet. I'm more likely to cry "foul" and declare how unfair life is. I am more likely to do all those things because as a human being I don't want to go through the painful experience. I don't want to go through something that in the long run may make me a better person. It is part of the human experience to want to bypass spiritual growth, yet part of the condition as a spiritual being to transcend through such experiences. That's our job. I've learned to accept this, and as a result, life has become much easier to maneuver.

After some internal debate I've decided to let you in on some of my own personal traumas that I have weathered in life. These were troubling times that caused such growing pains that I needed to journal as a means of freeing myself from the source of pain, in order clarify and open myself up to the lesson. As such, contained within this book are some excerpts from journal entries. The decision to use a journal entry is due to the raw honesty that would be diluted if I were to rewrite the entries. I have shared my uncensored, inner thoughts because I believe that some may benefit from the realization that they are not alone, or perhaps are better off. Most people, when asked, would rather keep their own problems than trade for someone else's problems. There is hope, regardless of your own personal situation. There is a path out. That path begins with honesty, open-mindedness, and willingness to change. The path is also a lot easier to walk if you appreciate the humor that can be embraced along the way.

*Journal Entry: <u>I Know I'm in Trouble When…</u>*

Depression has become such a familiar presence in my life that it is almost a norm. But for 2 years of blissful normalcy, I have been on anti-depressant medication for most of my adult life. I've learned how to work with depression, when to take it seriously and when to become one with it. When I say "become one" what I mean is that since depression is more the norm than the exception, it is really no cause for alarm. "Oh, I'm depressed… and?…and what?…so what?…continue on, do the next thing that's in front of you. Live, anyway."

There are little signs to tell me that I need to monitor the severity of depression. For example, when I wake up in the morning and I have no idea what day it is. I will sit there for a few moments and search my mind to determine the actual day. Is it the weekend? Is it a work day? Regardless of the day, I have this overwhelming sense of "I can't. I just can't get out of bed. I can't face another day." If it is a work day there is almost a sense of dread, because it will require energy to put on my "public face." You know that "face." The one that smiles and tells the world: "Hi, I have it together. Nothing wrong here. Just going about my day." Most of the time this is a good thing because it gets me outside myself and focused on whatever task is at hand. It's a mild symptom, a little warning sign, when I wake up in the morning with a feeling of dread.

If the episode of depression continues I notice that my taste in music changes rather dramatically. Normally, I am "in concert" when I travel in my truck. I have a CD on and I just sing to my heart's content. I have been told that I have a nice voice, and my response is usually: "Well, that's a good thing because I love to sing and I'm going to whether it sounds good or not." Singing moves energy in a very healing manner. It just doesn't matter what kind of song it is. Whether it is a sad song, an angry song, a happy song, or a seductive song, there is a song for any mood, and the music helps me to work through or with the emotion that I am feeling. Depression is stagnation. Music moves the depression to a higher energy frequency.

Another warning flag goes up when I don't want to hear any lyrics at all, only music. If I only want to hear classical music, I know that my depression is something that must be monitored closely. Don't misunderstand. I have a full appreciation for classical music. I have often wondered if I was an accomplished violinist in another life. It's as though I can feel the instrument in my arms. I can almost play along, knowing the note that will come next and feeling "at one" with the instrument. There is an intense passion that almost hurts, as if a wave of grief comes over me. I find no meaning in the paradox, other than the music makes me feel alive and mournful at the same time. When I yearn for classical, I know that I am going within. I know that there is a deep, dark void that is like a vacuum. As I travel into the "Black Hole" I become intolerant of any music. I think to myself: "No music. No sound." Silence is essential. Silence is essential because there is too much noise in my head. I yearn for numbness. Days, sometimes weeks, will go by with no music, no radio, no CD's, no sound, no singing. No life. The vibrations of life are too intense. No music is a serious warning sign, and an indicator that I will be in trouble if I don't take some sort of action.

I lose my appetite. Nothing interests me. Food doesn't taste as good. Eating is a chore that I want no part of. Even chocolate and ice cream don't interest me. This rarely concerns me, because even if I lose weight (as I have in the past) I know that I will put it back on. My weight fluctuates 10-20 pounds, depending on my mental status. I have different sizes of clothing for whatever place I'm at. Seinfeld once did an episode on how things always seem to balance out. That's how I feel about weight gain and weight loss. It's happened before, it will happen again, it will all even out. Never mind the havoc it creates for my metabolism, blood glucose, energy level, immune system. I've learned to live with that as well.

Sleep patterns change dramatically when I enter the "Black Hole." I have often told people that I was "born tired." I'm tired almost all the time. If I sit still for more than ten minutes, I can fall asleep. Forget sitting. If I stand still for more than ten minutes I can fall asleep. I've fallen asleep on bus benches, on the floor in a department store, while waiting in line at the grocery store, during class, watching television, on buses, trains, at work, and believe it or not, standing in line in the middle of Grand Central Station during rush hour. Sleeping is not a problem. When I make it to my bed at night, it probably takes only seconds to fall asleep. I'm out like a light, and not even a major electric storm will wake me ("Did you hear the thunder last night?" "What thunder?"). Apparently, I don't move very much while I'm sleeping, either. I get what I affectionately call "bed injuries." A 'bed injury' occurs when I sleep in one position for so long that a muscle strain occurs. For example, when I sleep on my side I must put a lot of pressure on my back because I wake up with an incredible sharp pain between my shoulder blades that lasts for days. I'll wake up with a stiff neck because I didn't move for hours at a time. Weird, huh? Whatever.

Anyway, when sleeping becomes a problem it is a major indicator that the depression is getting deep. I wake up (wide awake) at 1:00 am and cannot fall back asleep for hours. Then I play the "is it time to wake up" game. I'll lie there, trying to relax, focusing on my breathing and occasionally looking at the clock. "Is it time yet?, Nope, its 2 am…3am…4am." During this time frame it's as if someone gave me a shot of adrenalin. I am ready for the Super Bowl. Not tired at all, ready to start cleaning, thinking, thinking, thinking. The only reason I don't get up is because I'm afraid of how tired I will be the next day. This sleeping pattern can go on for days and weeks. It is draining, and eventually brings me to the next level in the Black Hole.

Believe it or not, all of this is tolerable. Not comfortable, and certainly not what I prefer, but it is tolerable. What is not tolerable is how depression affects my mind and my soul. With regard to my soul, it is as if suddenly there is no will to live. There will be waves of dysphoria throughout the day. The wave almost has the same sensation as an elevator when it drops on the way to a lower floor. There is this 'falling sensation' or maybe 'free-falling' sensation that I get in elevators. I know I'm going down, fast, and I can only hope that the elevator is functioning properly because it feels like it's going to crash. Then the elevator slows to an airy stop. All anxiety dissipates. The same kind of sensation occurs with the waves of depression that come over me. I've had many years to conduct a "self-study," if you will, and there are no external factors that trigger this sensation. It's like a chemical reaction, a wave, which has no tangible cause. 'The Wave' is not a good thing. It is an indicator that if I don't have my medication evaluated I am going to be in trouble. It's as if my soul, my spirit, my essence, is falling.

I know I'm in trouble. I know, and I have outbursts of tears, for I am afraid that I will be discovered. God forbid anyone should know how dysfunctional I can become. Enter the tricks of the mind. Let the games begin. Initially, when depression starts to rear its ugly head, I become rather philosophical. It is exuberating and exhilarating. My mind travels all over the place with very intricate theories. I get this sensation that I am connected with the Universe. It is as if I have tapped into The Truth, the Oneness, as if I have a knowledge and understanding of questions that many will never dream of answering. There is a knowing. I am of this earth-plane and of the spirit-plane at the same time. There is so much knowledge and wisdom to tap into. It occurs in an instant. In a flash, all these truths unfold. It is not unlike one of the opening scenes in <u>A Beautiful Mind</u>, when John Nash is looking at how light is fragmented through the drinking glasses, creating a pattern that matches another student's tie. John Nash sees the mathematical theory. My mind is not mathematical, yet the concept is similar in that there is an unfolding and a moment of Truth. My mind does this all day, for days on end. I listen and I hear and I know and I understand. And then, like classical music, there is a tremendous pain in 'the knowing' for it reminds me of my existence here on earth. It reminds me of the Human Condition and the task before me. I am not of the spirit world. I am of the earth. I am in this body, trudging through the road of life.

Now there is a painful reality, a painful awareness. I become incredibly sensitive. I will be in my truck driving down the highway, and grieve at the sight of land being cleared for development. "Do they not know what they are doing to the delicate balance that nature provides?" I grieve for the trees being cut down and chopped into mulch; the very trees that took decades and centuries to grow. The trees that provided oxygen, shade, shelter, housing for animals, beauty, and majesty. I grieve at the fact that man is too busy building to consider allowing a tree to stand, to consider working around the tree, to even consider transplanting it. If we can go to the moon, why can't we save the trees? I grieve for the animals that are displaced. That was their "development" that they lived in for generations. "Do they not know that there are families, young ones, infants living on that land? Animals are the custodians of the earth. How can we displace them?" Isn't "displace" a kind word? 'Displace' harbors us from the harsh realities of the bulldozers and machines of mass destruction. We kill in the name of progress. As I drive by these clearing fields I grieve deeply in my soul. I want to retreat, to escape to the mountains where I cannot see and experience the "progress" of man. It is almost unbearable, and it is also a reality of procreation.

Even more painful is the sight of the victims of progress that lie on the side (or middle) of the road. How is it that so many drivers do not see an animal attempting to cross the road? I just don't get it. Is it that the driver doesn't care, is it a game (like target practice), is it slow reflexes, poor driving skills, ignorance? What? The answer is of no consolation to me. I see every one of those bodies on the road. I hope and pray that death came quickly and with mercy. It is such a tragedy to me. Between the 'public urban developments' and the 'hit and runs' I find myself having a difficult time driving. I am aware of the development of man when I am not depressed; however, when I am depressed the bereavement is almost overwhelming. I compensate by looking at the reality of the situation. I didn't cause this. I didn't do this. I can't stop this. God hasn't intervened so who the hell am I? The way I figure it, God and I will grieve together, knowing that it is a consequence of man's free will. There is a Purpose, a Higher Order, to all of this. I see it, I grieve it, and I give myself permission to allow it to be as it shall be. I give thanks, I apologize for man's atrocities ('they know not what they do'), and I have some peace.

Are we having fun yet? My mind triumphs in revelations and mourns the deeds of humankind when I reach this stage of depression. It is like a rollercoaster, with twists and turns. I am constantly thinking, until the time comes when the thinking is agitating. It's too much noise on the inside now, not just on the outside. There's too much stimuli. My mind becomes a maze of truth and deception and I can't find my way. Sometimes I feel this tingling sensation and I can feel my body shrinking and then getting large again. I feel like I'm in orbit, with no gravity. My body is floating at angles as I am shrinking and becoming my normal size again, like a lens on a telephoto lens that is close-up and then distant.

This tends to progress to seeing shadows dart by out of the corner of my eye. ("What was that?") Sometimes the shadows are like dots; sometimes they are like dark streaks, sometimes like black shooting stars. This will progress to 'seeing' animals darting or dashing around. Sometimes I see rats or mice, sometimes raccoons or opossums, sometimes a dog or a cat. The thing is that for a split second I really see them. They are there one moment and they seem to vanish the next moment. They appear behind furniture, under cars, in hallways, when people are around, and when I'm alone. They are there, and I know at this point that I am hallucinating, yet at the same time what I see is very real. I've seen other things, too. I used to feel blood trickling down my arms onto my wrists (as if I had cut myself or had been cut by someone). The bleeding was almost a comfort. "Finally, something tangible to validate my pain."

There are other kinds of hallucinations. I was sitting in my office one day. There was an oil painting of a seaport hanging on the wall. I wasn't looking at the painting, but out of the corner of my eye I saw the boats in the picture bobbing in the harbor. I was a bit startled and looked again only to find the boats were still bobbing. The phone cord curled up at that moment. Things were moving that shouldn't have been moving. The picture on the wall was a bit disconcerting, because I was sitting there really seeing the ocean move and the boats bob. It was real. It was also time to go home. As I turned out of the parking lot and drove down the road, I was struck by the magnificent beauty of the mountainous terrain. The sun was setting, and the skyline was orange. It was like a scene from Montana or Utah. These were big bold mountains, with cumulous clouds floating about. I was completely awestruck. My thought was: "My God, these mountains are gorgeous." Almost as quickly as I had the thought, another thought followed: "I live in Florida. There are no mountains in Florida. There aren't even hills in this area." The mountains remained for a few more moments, and then disappeared. Hello? Even the queen of denial can't ignore that one. Time to get help. Time for medication.

For those with a background in psychology, I know it must sound like I meet several criteria for Bipolar Disorder. Good differential diagnosis, yet there are so many more to consider. Am I Bipolar, Schizophrenic, Psychotic Disorder NOS (not otherwise specified), or maybe it's Major Depression with psychotic features? How about PTSD, Dissociative Identity Disorder, Depersonalization? While I experience criteria for all of these disorders, I assure you I was not all of those things. In fact, after over ten years of therapy a correct diagnosis was finally made by a very talented therapist who referred me to another talented therapist who had the knowledge and experience to treat me. Anti-depressant medication does alleviate the symptoms. The only problem is that they work for a while, and then stop working. Then it's time to "tweak" the meds again.

At any rate, these are the symptoms that I have become aware of over the years that let me know when I'm in trouble. I was thinking about that one day and realized that if I don't choose to be in denial, ("I am not mentally ill and I don't need medication.') then I know the signs to respect and address. I know I'm in trouble when…

## Addendum

This was written some time in 2002. At the time of this writing (2010) I have been medication free for approximately six years. In fact, my depression has been in remission most of that time. When symptoms reappeared, I was able to manage the depression without going back on medication. I attribute this to the years of therapy I have had, to working an active recovery program through a Self-Help Program, to disputing irrational beliefs, to regular exercise, and to continued spiritual development through the works of such great modern-day thinkers as Wayne Dyer, Eckhart Tolle, Deepak Chopra, Elizabeth Kubler-Ross, Caroline Myss, Stephen Hawking, Louise Hay, Rhonda Byrne, Gary Zukov, Viktor Frankl, Thich Nat Hahn, David Hawkins, Sylvia Browne, Brian Weiss, M.D., Charles Whitfield, M.D., Shirley MacClaine, and Melissa Etheridge (Listen to The Awakening, 2007, Island Records, and you will know what I mean) . Indeed, for the first time in my life I have been medication free and depression free. I feel like I have reached the 'land of the free', the land of the functioning. I not only value life, I enjoy life. This is truly a miracle that I am grateful for on a daily basis. I included this chapter to send out a message of hope for those who still suffer from the grips of a mental health disorder. There is hope. There is life. There is joy.

The National Institute of Mental Health (NIH) provided the following statistics for 2010: approximately 20.9 million Americans (9.5% of the population) meet criteria for a mood disorder. Of that number, 14.8 million Americans (6.7%) meet criteria for Major Depressive Disorder.[1,2] The NIH goes on to report that Major Depressive Disorder is the leading cause of disability among Americans age 15-44[3].

In order to be diagnosed with a mood disorder, or any psychiatric disorder for that matter, one needs to meet certain criteria, and those criteria need to severely limit a person's ability to function. Even when an individual meets criteria for a disorder, the way that the disorder "translates" in any given person is slightly different. In other words, not all depressed people have the exact same symptoms. Likewise, I can put twenty alcoholics in one room and while they may all meet diagnostic criteria, they will have different stories and varying degrees of symptoms. Illness is a personal expression, even though there are shared commonalities that make up any given diagnosis. This is a partial explanation for why medications do not act the same on everyone. A medication that is a God-send for one person may cause debilitating adverse effects for another. In the psychiatric field, finding the best medication is not an exact science. Indeed it can be more like trial and error. Medication can assist in providing the proper balance of brain chemistry. It can be life saving. It can also be overprescribed.

The pharmaceutical industry has strong lobbying power and is adept at influencing politicians, physicians, and consumers. We live in a day and age when many patients expect some form of medication for a quick fix of an illness. There is a balance between body, mind, and spirit that generates health. Mental illness occurs on a continuum. There is a small percentage of the population that needs medication on a daily basis throughout their entire lives in order to function, and/or be kept safe from harm or from hurting others. There is a larger percentage of the population that requires medication for a temporary period in their lives in order to help them correct a chemical imbalance in the brain while they do the work of strengthening their body, mind, spirit through proper nutrition, exercise, counseling, and social/spiritual support.

The vast majority of the population does not require medication. I am not "against" medication, as medication is essential for some and helpful to others. At the same time, there are benefits to utilizing exercise, nutrition, counseling, and social supports to weather the storms of life—rather than take a pill. Many addicts and alcoholics in recovery are frequently prescribed medications that are contraindicated; which simply means that the medications prescribed frequently trigger a relapse that all too often results in their going back to their drug of choice. Physicians, psychiatrists, dentists, etc do not receive enough training in substance use disorders to know which medications are contraindicated for alcoholics and addicts in recovery. It gets even more complicated for those with co-occurring disorders (the presence of a substance use disorder and a mental health disorder). Addicts and alcoholics in recovery can better protect themselves by consulting with an addictions specialist about medications that are "safe" and those that could trigger a relapse. The goal is not to go against medical advice or dictate one's own treatment, but to collaborate with professionals in order to provide continuity of care.

1. Kessler RC, Chiu WT, Demler O, Walters EE. Prevalence, severity, and comorbidity of twelve-month DSM-IV disorders in the National Comorbidity Survey Replication (NCS-R). *Archives of General Psychiatry*, 2005 Jun; 62(6):617-27.
2. U.S. Census Bureau Population Estimates by Demographic Characteristics. Table 2: Annual Estimates of the Population by Selected Age Groups and Sex for the United States: April 1, 2000 to July 1, 2004 (NC-EST2004-02) Source: Population Division, U.S. Census Bureau Release Date: June 9, 2005. http://www.census.gov/popest/national/asrh/
3. The World Health Organization. *The global burden of disease: 2004 update*, Table A2: Burden of disease in DALYs by cause, sex and income group in WHO regions, estimates for 2004. Geneva, Switzerland: WHO, 2008. http://www.who.int/healthinfo/global_burden_disease/GBD_report_2004update_AnnexA.pdf.

# CHAPTER TWO

# AMAZING GRACE

*During the late 1980s I worked for the county as an addictions counselor in residential and outpatient settings. During that time, there were some "never" promises that I silently made to myself. One was that I would "never" work with the mentally ill. Another was that I would "never" work on a Detox Unit. The final "never" was that I would "never" work with those involved with the criminal justice system. These were absolutes, and seemingly logical decisions. In my biased mind, anyone with a criminal background engaged in willful misconduct. I wanted nothing to do with them. I wanted to work with people that wanted help. With regard to working on a Detox Unit, if you've ever been on one then you know that these patients are compromised by medication and are typically too occupied with withdrawal symptoms to be able to completely focus on recovery. The severely mentally ill were, it seemed to me, beyond help. Their mannerisms were frightening, their behavior unpredictable, their intellect compromised by delusions. Clearly, these three populations were not for me. I was too young to realize that when I set down such "absolutes" I was actually charting my next lessons. Of course, I ended up working with all three populations. Each "never" line that I crossed provided the catharsis needed for both personal and professional growth. They were the best experiences of my life. They were personal challenges to overcome and in each case, my clients gave me more than I ever could have given them.*

I was desperately in need of employment. The classifieds offered few options. There was an ad for a community mental health center that had an opening in the dual diagnosis unit. This agency always had available positions and it was known by all that this was due to the fact that the salary was very low. Taking a position with this agency would mean a $12,000 pay cut, as well as working with the persistently severe mentally ill. I didn't know what was worse: the pay cut or the 'chronically and persistently severe mentally ill.' The fact was I desperately needed a job. My unemployment benefits were running out, and I needed to find something soon. Knowing that I was backed into a corner, I made the call and set up the interview.

As I pulled into the parking lot I was relieved at the sight of a brand new building. Somehow I had imagined a dark musty unkempt building to house the mentally ill. The grounds were beautifully landscaped and the building was clean and bright. As I entered the building I heard a lot of noise. It was a cacophony of sounds. As much as I wanted to canvas the area to see where all these strange sounds were coming from, it became evident to me that I was the 'stranger in the building' and was getting stared at. Someone said "Hi" and I wanted to bolt back to my car. Somehow I made it the supervisor's office where I was to have my interview. She was in the middle of a crisis situation and had to excuse herself as soon as I walked into her office. She asked me to have a seat, stating that she'd be 'back in a few minutes.' Those 'few minutes' felt like an eternity. I had to talk myself into staying for the interview. It was clear to me that this was not the place for me. Was I crazy? I couldn't work here. People were loud. They talked nonsense. They were crazy. I couldn't see this working out. I could literally hear people talking to themselves. Some were making animal sounds. How could I do therapy with those people? By now it was clear to me that I could have run from the building two or three times without getting caught. I was determined to save face and at least get through the interview. I kept trying to reassure myself that the interview would be a good experience—good practice for the next job that was truly meant for me. The supervisor returned and, of course the interview went well and, of course, I was offered the position. I have never been so angry and so distressed at being offered a job. I was in crisis. I would have rather been offered a job cleaning septic tanks.

My first week of employment was depressing. I would lock myself in my office and stare out the window onto the courtyard. The unit I was assigned to was for those with a diagnosis of mental illness and chemical dependence. The clients on this unit had a higher level of functioning than the clients in the rest of the building. These clients would attend the program from 9am-1pm and then return either to a group home or family member's home for the remainder of the day. It was a Day Treatment program, and clients remained in this program up to four years. The goal was to assist them in developing the skills needed to maintain employment while living in a supervised environment. Some of them were functional enough to have the ultimate goal of living independently. Most would require disability benefits throughout life.

When I ventured out of my office to 'engage' with the clients I was struck by the lack of spontaneity. They were like little soldiers. Maybe even more like automatons. There seemed to be no expression, no vitality. No laughing. No resistance. No acting out. Addicts act out. I was used to that. I wasn't used to little soldiers doing as they were told. There was this veil of medication that made them all so flat. No emotion. I would retreat to my office in tears. The tears were for the grief I felt for these people. What kind of life was this? It didn't seem fair. The tears were also for me, because I felt sorry for myself for needing this job.

During that first week, I would stare out my window and watch a client who I came to refer to as 'the sweeper.' He would sweep all day. He'd arrive at the facility and sweep from one end of the building to another. It was an active, quick, compulsive, and repetitive, "sweep, sweep, sweep." He did this for four hours, only breaking a half hour for lunch. He swept so hard and so fast that his clothes were soaked through with sweat in no time at all. His sweeping wasn't proficient, as the dirt would just be pushed from one place to another. I was disgusted that the helping professionals of this facility would allow such a thing to occur, as it appeared cruel and an abuse of labor. I was truly appalled and voiced my concern to a colleague. When I asked her why the psychiatrist didn't put him on medication, her response took me back. The fact was that he was not only on medication, but that it was the highest dose possible. The Sweeper was functioning better than he ever had in his life. He had a violent history, and I was warned not to let him touch me. ("If he comes near you say: "NO TOUCHING!") His compulsive sweeping was a re-channeling of aggressive compulsions. He was doing well. I on the other hand, was not, and continued to ask myself what I was doing there.

I retreated even more to the safety of my office. I would stare out that window for hours, wondering what I was going to do and praying for guidance from a Higher Power.

While in a meditative trance the phone rang. I heard a woman's voice say: "What are you doing?" I was a bit taken aback, and inquired who this was and what she meant. There was also some paranoia building within, as I wondered how long I had been watched and even made a quick look around the room to see if there were cameras in my office. She said she was a counselor from the 'other side' of the courtyard and saw me staring out the window all the time. She wondered what I was doing. I could only respond by saying: "Meditating." She laughed and made some comment about maintaining sanity that way. We chatted for a few minutes before she let me off the hook. I was appalled. I felt like I was caught in a most vulnerable moment. Now I was in a double-bind. My office was no longer 'safe' and it wasn't 'safe' outside my office. I was forced into a choice: resign or surrender to my insecurities. I was finally ready to receive the lesson. The student was now ready, and as a result my teachers began to appear.

I made a decision to be the counselor that I was accustomed to being. I am very animated when I teach. I use humor. I engage clients. I thrive on moments during a group when I see a light of insight shine in a client's eyes. Those moments mean that someone has been reached, touched, understood. Those moments have the potential to unleash hope. Those are the magical moments that inspire miracles, both big and small. I needed to know if these clients could be reached. I needed to know if I could touch their souls. I knocked, and they let me in. In no time this group became animated. They laughed, they cried, they worked through anger. They connected with and internalized this concept of recovery. It was not about behaving. It was about living. It was about connecting.

Betty was a large African American woman in her twenties. She was diagnosed with paranoid schizophrenia. She was also cocaine dependent. To further complicate her treatment, Betty was diabetic. As most clients who were newly admitted to the unit, Betty was 'marginally stable.' Her medication compromised her ability to think clearly. Her thoughts were slow, her movements were slow, and she appeared paranoid. Compared to the others on the unit, she was very unstable. Betty was assigned to my caseload. Her paranoia made it difficult for me to connect with her. She was isolative and withdrawn, and she said she didn't want to be a part of our unit. One day Betty was missing, which was difficult to imagine because the clients had only two rooms that they used during the day. In fact, clients were not permitted to go anywhere unless they asked permission first. It was the staff's job to know where the client's were at all times. It was like Betty was there one minute and gone the next. None of the clients knew where she was. An all out search was launched. When it became clear that Betty could not possibly be in the building, we extended our search to a 7-11 that was down the street. Betty had been sighted there, and was again missing. After a good thirty minutes of running all over the place, Betty was finally found walking back from the store. She giggled at our concern, reporting that she became thirsty and went for a soda. This woman was like a very large slow moving vehicle, and yet for some thirty minutes she had been invisible. We laughed with her as to how she had managed to move quicker that day than an entire staff. She had meant no malice, and promised not to leave without permission ever again. She kept her promise, and gradually became receptive to the support offered by the staff and her peers.

As Betty became more stable, she began to trust me. She confided in me about the love she felt for her 7 year old son, and how she wanted nothing more in the world than to have a home for the two of them. She was living with her mother and her siblings, in an environment that was sometimes hostile and unsupportive.

Betty was a joy to work with. She had a beautiful smile and a wonderful laugh. She was really beginning to invest in the program when something started to go wrong. We had a barbeque at a local park the day before, which turned out to be a great time for all. Betty appeared in my office the next morning and said: "Miss Vickie, I'm mad at you." When I asked her why, she stated: "Because you put poison in my hamburger yesterday. I know you really didn't, that it's my sickness, but I know that you did. I'm mad at you." By now I was accustomed to this kind of statement, and it meant nothing more than Betty needed a medication adjustment. Betty agreed, and we called the psychiatrist for an immediate appointment. Normally, this would clear up the problem, and the schizophrenia would go back into remission. While talking to the psychiatrist, Betty said that she did not want to take her medication any more. She wanted to attend church instead. To my complete amazement, the psychiatrist agreed with her. This was later confirmed by the psychiatrist himself, who told me that Betty found our program too stressful and would respond well to church.

The fact that a psychiatrist would collude with a patient experiencing active psychosis, recommending church instead of medication and treatment, was beyond comprehension. I attempted to contact Betty by telephone at her home. She refused to talk to me. In fact, she refused to come back to treatment. Her case manager made a home visit, appealing with Betty to come back to treatment. Betty agreed to visit with the psychiatrist. I was able to see her briefly in the hallway, and she assured me that she was doing well. She said her toe had been infected and the psychiatrist told her it was healing. I looked at the toe, and was aghast, as it was gangrenous. Betty became angry when I suggested she have a physician look at the toe. She turned and walked away, refusing to get help and refusing to speak with me. I spoke with the psychiatrist, who told me the toe "was healing." I went to my supervisor, and then to my supervisor's supervisor. I tried to get the case manager involved, believing that she may have more political power than me. It was clear to me that Betty was in danger. She was unable to care for herself, and needed to be hospitalized in order to save her life. No one would listen, and who could blame them. I was going up against a psychiatrist, an M.D., and all I had at the time was a Bachelor's Degree. Who was I to question authority? I was an alarmist in everyone's mind. On more than one occasion I went up to and against authority, appealing that they hospitalize Betty and warning that she would be dead in two weeks if she didn't get medical attention. Again, no one would listen.

About 10 days passed without hearing from or seeing Betty. I was on my way to the group room for our morning meeting. The door was open a crack, and as I peered in I saw the group standing in a circle holding hands. Betty was in the middle of the circle, singing Amazing Grace. Her voice was strong and beautiful, yet exquisitely delicate. It was a moment when time stood still, when nothing mattered but what was going on in the presence of that circle. Betty was saying goodbye. She was singing her song, and everyone in that room knew it. There was a moment of silence when she finished. As a staff member, I was going to have to ask her leave because she was no longer a member of our program. It pained me to uphold such a boundary, when I knew all too well the importance of this moment. As I began to speak, Betty quietly interrupted with: "I know, it's ok. I'm leaving now." As was customary, I escorted Betty out of the building. I did not say a word and kept my distance, as she had not spoken to me in well over a week and had clearly seen me as "the enemy." I did not want to upset or escalate her. I just wanted her to be able to leave as quietly as she had come in. Before reaching the door, Betty turned toward me, looked me in the eyes, and peacefully whispered: "I love you, Miss Vickie." I responded with: "I love you, Betty." She left without another word.

Two days later, the case manager informed me that Betty had died at home in her sleep. The cause of death was from blood sepsis- a direct result from the gangrene. It was almost two weeks to the day that I had warned the agency and pleaded for her hospitalization. Being right didn't feel good. I was enraged and sick inside. I was also thankful for the gift that she gave me. Betty made her peace, was at peace, and in her own loving way left this world with the kind of Grace that I can only hope to emulate. She taught me that the most important thing is not necessarily 'being right'. Sometimes it is more important to allow someone to walk their path. It's not always about saving lives and souls. Sometimes it's about loving enough to let go.

# CHAPTER THREE

# CRIMINAL "JUSTUS"

I laid in bed listening to the clock radio. A feeling of dread washed over me as I thought about rising to meet the challenge of my first day on the job. Treatment Alternatives to Street Crimes, TASC, was a program that was housed in the county jail. The thought of going inside a jail, let alone working there, was daunting to me. How did I get myself into this mess? This was clearly a mistake. I lured myself out of bed by promising myself that I would only keep the job until I found something else.

The building was "institutional beige" both inside and out. There is no welcoming committee when you work at the jail. In fact, newcomers are looked at with skepticism and, as I was to find out, disdain. The question is, how long will you last? The reality is, probably not very long. I was escorted around the facility my first few days on the job. My supervisor provided me with the initial tour, but it was my colleagues that really gave me the orientation I needed to assimilate in this new environment. It did not take long to realize that working in the jail was going to be a daily assault on my senses. As I mentioned, the color was very drab. The walls may as well have been gray. In addition, there are no windows in a jail to let natural light in. As a result, the lighting from the institution contributed to that "closed in" feeling. Each corridor offered a different offensive smell that ranged from feces, to urine, to cleaning chemicals, to body odor, to whatever it was that they were cooking that day. In fact, the cafeteria hallway was quite often the foulest smelling corridor in the facility. The sounds could be deafening at times, especially when detainees would erupt into a cacophony of whistles, grunts, and cat-calls when we entered a cell block. At other times, it was the deafening sound of the steel door slamming behind me that would echo in the silence of the hallway. Working in the jail was much like being sentenced to jail. The only difference was that I got to go home at night.

The corrections officers let me know how they felt about my presence almost immediately. Within my first few days I was asked by one of the officers what my position was at the jail. When I told him that I was a TASC counselor, the response was: "Oh great, another bleeding heart." I tried to explain my purpose and philosophy, and quickly understood that I was wasting my breath. I got a brief lecture on the criminal population and how I was in the "wrong place" to be helping people. What followed over the next six months was akin to a hazing period. The corrections officers were like a tightly knit brotherhood, of which I did not belong. It appeared to me that they were doing their best to run me out of the jail. On one occasion, I was in the cell where the TASC clients were housed. I was facilitating a group, when the doors opened and the officer stepped in (interrupting my group) to deliver toilet paper. He began throwing rolls of toilet paper to the detainees. One of the rolls nearly hit me in the head. As it grazed past my ear, a detainee commented on the forcefulness of the throw. The officer smiled. I remained silent. On another occasion, an officer was on the second floor of the cell doing a "routine inspection," while I was on the first floor. He "accidentally" dropped a mattress within inches of me. Frequently, I was left waiting at locked doors. It was a reminder to me that "they" controlled when and if I was going to get out. I always kept my cool, and acted as though I was not bothered by their gestures. In actuality, I was both fearful and enraged. The key to my survival was in not letting them know this. I guess this aggravated them on some level, as the final "test" could have been disastrous for me.

I was in a cell block that was one of the worst in the jail. The men in this cell typically had violent records, and generally were not appropriate for the TASC program. Despite this, I was required to interview a detainee from this section of the jail. This particular block was a long corridor of about six cells on each side. A corrections officer sat in a chair in the middle of the corridor, and there was an enclosed area of officers at the end of the corridor. Normally, there were two sets of doors to the cells in this block. The inside set was a set of doors with bars. The outside set was solid steel. The bars would close on the inside of the cell, and then the steel doors would open—giving access to the detainees. On this particular day, the officers buzzed me into a cell that housed about 40 detainees. The steel doors opened, and as I stepped into the cell to talk through the bars, the steel doors closed. This was not supposed to happen. The steel doors were supposed to remain open. Then, as I noticed that this particular cell had no panic button or speaker system, the doors with the bars started to open. Within seconds I was alone in a cell with 40 male detainees, two of which were to my immediate left and right, taking showers. I could not have been in a much more vulnerable position. One of the detainees was kind enough to advise me that the corrections officer who was normally stationed in the middle of the corridor had just walked away. Another detainee was kind enough to state the obvious: "Ma'am, it's not safe for you to be in here like this." These two men started banging on the steel doors to try to get the officers' attention. It seemed unlikely that this would work, as the officers were conveniently in the glass-enclosed office stationed out of view at the end of the hall. I heard someone say: "What are you going to do?" I played it cool, and said: "I have a TASC assessment to do, and that's what I'm going to do. If you want help, don't fuck with me. I need detainee _ _ _ _." The detainee approached me, and I went on with business as usual. Within minutes the doors with bars closed and the steel doors opened. On my way out, the officers met me at the end of the cell block and assured me that the incident was "an accident." I kept my composure and went about my day. I was never tested again.

I was grateful for the guardian angels that watched over me that day. What saved me were the men who tried to get the attention of the corrections officers. They took control of the situation. I was completely powerless, and everyone involved in that event knew it. Without those men, I'm sure I would have been a victim of a violent assault. I think that my composure was what put an end to the hazing period. Days after the incident, I was approached in the hallway by a senior officer, who asked me if I was FBI or CIA. Of course, I responded by saying that I couldn't tell him if I was. After that, the officers frequently asked me to fill out an application and become an officer. I suppose I passed all the tests and was accepted by the brotherhood. It allowed me to focus on my purpose, which was to distinguish the addict from the criminal, and to propose treatment as opposed to incarceration for the chemically dependent.

My exposure to those with a criminal history gave me an experiential rather than theoretical perspective on the levels of human functioning. There were essentially three levels, or subgroups, within the population of the jail. There was a subgroup of detainees who really were not criminals at heart. They were either mentally ill or chemically dependent (or both—which we call dually diagnosed) and had committed a crime typically related to their addiction or illness. Most of these individuals had charges of possession of drugs, drug paraphernalia, DUI, or petite theft. Some were incarcerated for the first time, while others were considered "habitual offenders." Many of them had never had treatment. They did not know how to change. They were stuck in a vicious cycle of addictive behaviors and consequences. They were lost and begging for help. These were the detainees for which I recommended community-based treatment.

The second subgroup of detainees was the career criminals. These individuals would meet criteria for a diagnosis of Antisocial Personality Disorder. They truly demonstrated no remorse for their crimes. The only palpable remorse was for the consequences of getting caught. These folks had previous convictions of grand theft, robbery, grand theft auto, drug trafficking. When asked why they stole a car, the most common answer was: "I needed it." This subgroup of detainees was manipulative, deceiving, dishonest, frequently clever, and almost always engaging or charming. Their primary motive was to "beat the system" and to get out of jail in the shortest time possible. They frequently espoused to "find God" and made empty promises of "changing for good." These were individuals who would spend their lives in and out of jail. These were the detainees that I was to spot and weed out. These were the detainees that would be referred to treatment programs while serving prison sentences.

The third subgroup was the sociopath. These were dark entities operating on a predatory level. Their crimes were violent and hideous. There was not only no remorse, but pleasure in the criminal acts perpetrated upon others. These were individuals who I came to realize needed to be locked up for life. There was no chance of rehabilitation for them. These people could not be helped, could not be reached. There was no shred of decency. This is a very small percentage of the population, and a percentage that most people fortunately never have to encounter. I quickly learned to move on when I was in the presence of a dark entity. I also learned which cell block they were likely to be housed in, and did not enter without a coworker. We affectionately donned this cell block "The Zoo" because the men in this block behaved like animals. Humor becomes a necessary tool for survival when you are in such an environment. (I've worked with wild and domestic animals throughout my life. Truth be told, animals behave much better than sociopaths.) I thick skin goes a long way, too. I was called more names than I could have ever imagined. After a while, it's just noise.

There were 28 men in the TASC cell that were hand-picked by the TASC counselors. While in our cell the clients received full substance abuse assessments, education groups, and case management. If they met certain criteria, we would go to court with them and recommend to the Judge treatment within the community (rather than incarceration). It was an immense responsibility that we did not take lightly. Our clients were challenged and put through many tests in order to earn our trust in their request for help. The TASC cell had the strictest rules of all the cells within the jail. This was serious business, and the clients responded in kind. These men thrived in an educational setting. They hungered for knowledge. They participated eagerly. Each morning I would arrive at the cell to facilitate group. The steel doors would open and all 28 men would be sitting at the steel tables awaiting my arrival. I had men of all colors and ethnic backgrounds, ages, and abilities. They all came together to generate a synergistic energy that created a powerful healing potential. It was a blessing to be a part of this process, to foster this synergism.

There was an education group that I facilitated on a monthly basis entitled "The Wall." The lesson was about identifying internal and external defense mechanisms that block healing and growth. The corrections officers thought I was out of my mind every time I did this group, as I would enter the cell with a book and lots of crayons in hand. The first time I facilitated "The Wall", the officers took one look at my crayons and told me I would never be able to get a bunch of adult male detainees to play with crayons. When I entered the cell

I felt looks of skepticism and insult coming from the men. I explained what I was going to do, assuring them that this was a powerful learning activity. Learning is not always about listening. In fact, we tend to learn on a deeper level when we involve as many of our senses as possible. I explained that I was going to read them a parable, complete with pictures. Their attention to detail was important, as at the end of the story we would be analyzing the parable to see how the principles of recovery were woven into the story. Once our discussion was complete, the men were handed a piece of paper and crayons, and instructed to draw their wall as it stood that day. In the process they were to identify the stones (or defenses) in their walls. Each man had a turn at presenting and describing his wall. It was a two-day group that was very powerful and enlightening to each group member. The deputies were always stunned at the amount of time the men spent on this assignment.

I was moved to tears (a rare occurrence) one day when the guys presented me with a keepsake. They all worked together on this project, providing input, while one of them made a caricature of me pulling one of them through his "wall." They advised me that day that I had "magic bullets"— that I had a way of getting to the core of an issue with the quickness of a bullet, and that the "bullet" was magic in that it had a healing influence on them. They expressed their gratitude at my presence in their lives. I couldn't possibly express how grateful I was to them. Their gift touched me deeply.

Some of the men were cognitively impaired as a result of their addiction. That's the professional way to say it. The guys in the cell taught me the street interpretation. There was one man, in particular, who could barely communicate. His stuttering was so bad that initially I thought it was an act. I was advised by the clients that he was "shot out." When I asked for clarification they explained that it was like his brain was "shot out"— meaning there was nothing left. So, "shot out" meant brain damaged from addiction. This particular man was "shot out" from huffing (sniffing) glue. It was pitiful because he really was there. There <u>was</u> something left. I saw the functioning brain. The problem was the glue huffing ruined his ability to verbalize his thoughts. There was a thinking man inside who couldn't communicate with the world. I let Kelly know that I knew this; that I heard him; that I saw him; that I would listen to him. I let him know this in front of the entire group. The group responded by extending themselves with patience. It could take Kelly up to five minutes to get a sentence or two out. We would wait. We would wait with all the time in the world. We heard him, and responded back, and Kelly began to reconnect with others. His ability to verbalize improved over time, although only slightly. The damage to the communication center of his brain was permanent, but the soul was able to heal. Kelly became a model client. His sincerity and gratitude were infectious. Kelly taught us that communication is more about the language of the soul than about the language of words. He taught me to look beyond the veil of brain trauma in order to find the spirit within.

There was another man who initially appeared beyond hope. His drug of choice was alcohol, and he was close to "wet brain." It took weeks for Aaron to be able to comprehend, to engage, to join life. We waited to see if he would come around, and slowly we saw the life come back into his eyes. He began to participate and improved beyond my expectations. He was warned repeatedly by the staff that he was at risk of permanent brain damage (Korsokoff's) if he went back to drinking. He was sentenced to treatment, and departed from our cell of sound mind and body. Six months later I received a request for services from Aaron. This meant, of course, that he had relapsed, was arrested, and was back in jail. I went to see Aaron to give him my thoughts on all of this and was taken aback at his condition. This man had crossed the line of no return. He did not recognize me, did not know he had been a TASC client only months before, and was not reality based. I checked on Aaron periodically, and his symptoms did not improve. It was jolting to witness such a transformation. It was a tragic reality that made an indelible impression upon me. I grieved the soul that was lost, and earned a new respect for the power of alcohol. This day, this moment, is really all that we have.

Jerry was another man with brain damage from alcohol. His level of functioning did not improve while he was in the TASC cell. However, he demonstrated a sincere desire for help. He was able to follow program structure, exhibited a desire to learn the basic principles of recovery, and had a kind heart that came shining through. Jerry was African American, and in his 50's. He was raised in poverty, dropped out of school, and turned to alcohol and cocaine to get by in life. Alcohol eventually damaged his brain. All of his charges were drug related. He had no history of violence. He had been arrested for possession of cocaine throughout his life (his only kind of charge) and each time he was sentenced to prison. This man never knew any other way. This was the first time in his life that he had heard of treatment or asked for help. He was the "perfect candidate" for TASC services, as he had never had treatment intervention. He desperately wanted help and had confidence that I would have him sentenced to treatment.

He had confidence because TASC services routinely obtained treatment for clients during sentencing disposition. Indeed, I had been successful in obtaining treatment for clients with more sordid criminal records. It was almost a sure thing that Jerry was to receive treatment, accept for the fact that his Judge was known to be "against treatment." Jerry was confident in my abilities, despite the Judge he was assigned to. On the day of his court hearing, he was like a little boy waiting to get the opportunity to go to school. He was just waiting for the final word, the permission to actually go to treatment. He was one of the last cases on the docket that day. I sat through case after case, and grew increasingly optimistic. The cases before the Judge were mostly habitual offenders with histories and arrests for charges much more severe than Jerry. Most of the men that went before the Judge that day received probation. In fact, the case before Jerry looked almost identical to his. This was a white male, in his fifties, with a history of possession of cocaine charges. The Judge sentenced him to probation. I was relieved and felt fairly confident. Jerry's case was called and things began to backfire quickly. The state's attorney was calling for five years prison time. The Judge was agreeing. The public defender was not defending. I was sworn in and began to testify on behalf of Jerry. I attempted to tell the Judge of TASC's assessment, observations, and recommendations. The Judge was not impressed, was not listening, and cut me off. The rest is a blur, although I believe I "rose to the occasion" and attempted to assert myself. I know I was threatened with contempt of court—probably about the time that I pointed out the obvious injustice of the sentence Jerry was about to receive compared with that of his white counterpart. The Judge dismissed me, and I sat helplessly as Jerry was sentenced to five years in Florida State Prison. Jerry looked across the courtroom at me in confusion. His confusion turned to anger, as he was escorted out of the courtroom. I knew that he did not understand what had transpired. He had dared to hope, and I had been the one to open the doorway to hope.

I walked out of the courtroom fighting back the tears. I was waiting for the elevator, feeling homicidal and suicidal, lamenting over the injustices of our society. The doors to the elevator opened, and my supervisor was standing there. It was the only time in a year and a half that we "bumped into each other" in the courthouse. It was a synchronistic event, another timeless moment in my life that I remember vividly. My supervisor was an African American male in his 50's. I told him what transpired and expressed my horror at the injustice that I had just witnessed. I verbalized that I was tired of seeing, over and over again, white men getting lesser sentences than black men. He remained calm and steadfast in the presence of my fury. I asked him how he could deal with this, and his quiet response caught me off guard. "You win some," he said, "you lose some." I exclaimed that this wasn't good enough, that it wasn't right, and that it wasn't fair. He went on to explain that it wasn't about what was fair or right. It was about the fight. It was about doing the footwork, and making a difference in the long run. We were agents of change, and in the process we would encounter injustice and unrighteousness. We were to be agents of change, anyway.

When I got back to the TASC cell I explained to the men what had transpired in court that day. Word had got back that I didn't help Jerry, and that he thought I was prejudice. The poor man didn't even realize that I was the only one fighting for him that day. We talked about prejudice, and how to overcome prejudice through positive change and growth. I invited them to not let any Judge have power over them ever again. They explained to me that day about the true meaning of Justice. I didn't get it at first. One of the guys wrote it out on a piece of paper. It read *JustUs*. "You know," he said, "Just Us whites." I got it. 'Just Us get Justice.' That was their reality, and the reality I had experienced that day. The deeper, underlying reality was that there was no color in our cell. We were one in what we were trying to do together. It was not a front, it was not an act. It was real. We were colorless. They let me in---black and white—because I let them in. All that was required was truth. Truths beget a spirit of love. That was something that no Judge could take away. There were many miracles in that cell. I was spiritually, mentally, and intellectually intimate with men in a way I never thought possible. I overcame my fear of men, my fear of criminals, and found out that I have more in common with men than I knew.

# CHAPTER FOUR

# BLESSED ARE THE CHILDREN

*Warning: This chapter includes stories about children that are disturbing. While these stories are not graphic in nature, some of their content explores life challenges when confronted with childhood death. If this is an issue that is too close to home for you, please skip this chapter and go on to the next.*

## The Gift of Compassion

Many, many years ago I was challenged by my own codependence and found it helpful to attend another one of those Self-Help Meetings. I had never been to this particular meeting and had arrived early. I sat in the back of the room while I waited for people to arrive. I heard my Spirit Guide, Tron, say "You are going to be asked to read." I found this highly unlikely, as I doubted the Chairperson would ask someone new to the meeting to read. I wasn't particularly in the mood, but decided that if I was asked, I would comply. The chairperson came in and began to set up for the meeting, asking people to do various tasks. She walked up to me and asked if I would mind doing one of the readings, and with a smile I accepted.

As people came into the room I watched them greet one another with warmth and compassion. A younger woman came in, with her infant, and the group almost spontaneously surrounded her. They were excited to see her and the baby, as she had apparently been away from the group due to the recent delivery of her infant. They were all very excited for her and she was smiling. I was across the room and out of view of this woman and her child. As the meeting started to get underway I suddenly felt overwhelmed with sadness. I knew that this child was gravely ill and probably wouldn't survive. I also knew that the mother of this infant knew this, and that she did not know if she could dampen all the happiness that she had just received by telling the group that her child may die. I knew that this woman was in a battle with herself as to what to do.

The meeting got underway, I did my reading, and a topic was provided. The group began its discussion and about halfway through the meeting the woman with the newborn raised her hand. She began by telling the group that she had been sitting there that whole time trying to decide what to do—that she wanted to tell the group the truth, but didn't know if she had the courage to do so because everyone was so happy for her. She went on to tell the group that shortly after the birth, her child had been diagnosed with some rare illness that had a very poor prognosis, and that the physicians were unsure if her child would survive.

The hair stood up on the back of my neck. Everything that I had perceived from the moment I had walked into that room had come true exactly as it had been revealed to me. My only comfort was that somehow this must have been in accordance with a Higher Order, for how else could I know such intimate details of this woman's moment in time. I sat there wondering why I had been given this information, and what I was supposed to do with it. I knew I could not heal this infant. I also knew that the "knowing" was there and had revealed itself to me. I decided to share this with the group, not to prove myself "psychic" but to hopefully provide comfort in the knowledge that the Universe was fully present and working in our lives. Sometimes we spend so much energy in the "why" and get stuck in a place of no resolution. Sometimes the answer is just "because." Knowing why doesn't reverse the trauma. Regardless of whether or not we know the reason, we are still left with the grieving. That is the task at hand, as arduous as that may be. Life can be cruel. I believe that it's not God that does these things to us. I believe that life does these things, and that God, angels, spirit guides, and other humans are present to support us through the storms in our life. The love for that woman in that meeting that day was not enough to heal her infant. It was enough to give her courage and support to make it through the day.

## The Gift of Life

Some years later, I was living in "Cracktown" in downtown Fort Lauderdale. Crack cocaine was certainly not the only drug in this area, but it was at the height of the crack epidemic. I lived in a spot in town that was a real housing potpourri. My street consisted of duplexes, the next street next to mine was Section-8 housing, and the streets adjacent to us were $400,000 homes. There were even some very charming homes built in the late 1800s/early 1900s that were very quaint. Part of this charm was a very old Firehouse that was still operating on a volunteer basis.

Across from my street was a house built in the very early 1900s. A woman lived there, with her two young children. The woman was probably in her 30's, although it was tough to guess at her age because she was clearly chemically dependent. Actually, I rarely saw this woman, but would hear her yelling at her two little girls to come in the house. I was always disturbed by this because these little girls were too young to be playing in the yard unattended. The oldest was about four years old and the other little girl was about two years old. The area was not safe for an adult to walk in, let alone for two little girls to be playing in. My concerns were in vain, as these were not my children and I was powerless over how this mother raised them. From time to time I would pause and watch these girls at play. I felt a dark energy in their world that they, especially the eldest, seemed to escape from during play. The older girl was very animated during play, and yet was always very attentive toward her younger sister. She seemed to be able to play and simultaneously baby-sit at such a tender age. I feared for what was in store for her as she grew older. I knew too much about addiction and how it impacts the children. I felt sadness for her and at the same time I delighted in her spirit. This one particular day she must have felt my loving intention for her as I was watching her play. She stopped what she was doing, turned to face me, smiled, and waved. I waved and smiled back. That was the only formal communication we ever had.

Two nights later I was getting into bed when I heard screaming. Now, screaming was normal in my crack neighborhood and after a while you just didn't hear it anymore. But this night was different. It was a death-curdling scream that sent me running out of the house in bare feet (I am never without shoes—even in the house, until I literally get into bed). I ran toward the end of the street and was horrified as I saw flames engulfing the house where the little girls lived. I don't mean a fire. I mean the entire front of the house was an orange blaze. The mother was in the middle of the street screaming: "My babies, my babies!!" The little girls were still in this two-story house! I ran to the mother and asked where in the house her children were. She did not know. I kept running until I reached the side door of the house, as I was determined to save those two beautiful girls. When I reached the side door what I encountered was nothing that anyone could have prepared me for. There was a black tornado of smoke that was impenetrable. This smoke was so thick, so ominous, that I instinctively knew that it meant instant death. There was no way that I could enter the house without dying. I just knew that trying was futile because I would never reach the children.

This was a significant moment for me because I have always believed that without even having to think about it, I would risk my own life to save a child. In fact, this is still true to this day. I know that I would just go into action and risk my own life, without hesitation. But this particular moment in time was a completely different situation. To even try meant death without the hope of reaching them. For most of my life I have wanted to die, prayed for death, and yet at this very moment a survival instinct kicked in that was completely invested in living. Until that moment I did not know that there was something inside of me that actually wanted to live. I was willing to die a hero, but not willing to die a martyr. To not even be able to try to save those two children was a most devastatingly helpless feeling.

Wanting desperately to save these little girls, I ran to the back of the house to see about a different entry point. There were about three African American males in their early 20's that had climbed to the second story to try to get in. They had broken the windows in an attempt to crawl into the house—only to find, just as I, that the smoke billowing from the house was impenetrable. I stood there and watched these young, tough, street-wise men cry as they gave up in the futility of the moment.

By this time the mother was frantic and began to run into the house. I, and a few others, grabbed her and held her. We all knew there was nothing anyone could do but wait for the fire department. The volunteer fire department was literally three houses down the street, but no one was actually at the fire house. We all stood there waiting for them to arrive. It took about 20 minutes for them to get there. Then we had to wait for them to suit up with their oxygen tanks in order to enter the house. Then, after the firefighters finally entered the house, we waited with the mother in a tight little circle and prayed. We all waited in a moment in time when black, white, young, old, addicted, non-addicted, criminal, non-criminal were all one in a desperate prayer for a miracle.

There are two sensory perceptions from that moment in time that are as vivid today as they were that terrible night. One was the stench of alcohol that was emanating from the mother of those two little girls. Her blood alcohol level must have been well over .15 from that all too familiar odor (A good part of my career has been working in Detox and Residential treatment settings). It was clear to me that she was alcoholic. The other sensory perception was the sound of a bell that rang constantly. Apparently, when the firefighters enter a hazardous situation there is a bell that rings constantly so that they can be found should they become incapacitated in the building. That bell rang loud and for what seemed like an eternity. By my best calculation at least 45 minutes had elapsed since I had run from my efficiency to the fire. I knew that the two little girls, if alive, were most likely in a coma and most likely would not survive. Too much time had gone by and with each passing minute my heart sank. Finally, the limp body of one of the little girls was passed out of the second story bedroom window, where the young black men had previously been trying to get in. Within seconds, the second lifeless body was passed through the same bedroom window. The girls had been found lying on the floor, by a bed, under a blanket. By the time the firefighters reached them it was too late. The girls had died from smoke inhalation.

News crews were all over the place. I knew a camera had been taping when I had restrained the mother. When the ambulance drove off the news reporters went into action. One of the local TV personalities was there and she was asking me questions. I asked to remain anonymous and told her what I knew off camera—which wasn't much. The fire made headline news—both locally and through CNN. I was hoping to find out information from the news about the cause of the fire. Instead, I kept hearing that bell ringing over and over and over again because that is what the news reels played. They also played the video of me restraining the drunk, screaming, frantic mother. I couldn't stop watching the news. It was comforting, and yet distressing—almost as though my psyche wanted to rewrite history by watching for a better outcome. It never came.

Investigators went throughout the neighborhood conducting interviews. I was able to learn that investigators initially suspected arson, and later ruled that out, determining that the fire started on the front porch. Apparently the mother had been smoking and left the house, allegedly to buy crack cocaine. She left her two little girls alone (something she had probably done many times before). The cigarette must have fallen and started the fire, which spread rapidly due to the age of the house. The mother was looking at criminal charges of neglect for the death of her children. I didn't follow the case after that. It was just too painful.

This was such a tragedy, such an incredible loss that can never be explained to any satisfaction. It was as it was. I had a lot of time to process this and try to make sense of it. I had certainly experienced a foreshadowing of this event. I had to wonder if these two little girls were saved from a wretched life of trauma. I had to wonder if these two little girls were only on this earth plane to teach us a lesson. Did they come together in this mission, to comfort one another—as they had literally accomplished this in life and in death? Did they come to teach the mother a painful, but necessary lesson so that she could evolve as a soul? Did they come to teach me that I actually valued my own life, to show me that deep within I wanted to live? For in my vain attempt to save their lives they gave me the gift of appreciation for my own. Did they come to show the world the sanctity of family, the value of life, the preciousness of our children? I will never forget the little girl with the spirit of love who stopped and waved at me that morning. It was as if she were saying 'hello' and 'goodbye.' There is no consolation but for the fact that she surely found eternal peace and love.

## *The Good Samaritan*

It was early Saturday morning and I was enjoying the peaceful sounds that nature makes as the day begins. At this time of morning there is the chirping of the cardinal and the woodpecker, as they begin to forage in trees. The air has a muffled quiet, simply because there are not enough people awake to generate the busy whirring noise that traffic constantly generates. Nature generates sounds. People make noise. In the midst of my morning bliss I heard in the distance a car skidding. The sound of this skid created an anxious anticipation as I waited for the moment of impact. At such moments, time seems to stand still—or at least be in slow motion. The main road was three houses away, and I was living in a wooded area so I could not see what was happening. I just had the sense of sound to advise me of what was transpiring. I heard the skid, the impact, and the sound of metal rolling over. I knew the vehicle had hit a tree or a telephone pole and rolled. Then I heard something that seemed impossible to hear, considering the distance that I was from the crash. I heard a loud expiration of breath. It was not a scream, and it wasn't really a groan or a sigh. This exhale was coming from a man, and it may have produced an "ugh" sound. It was the eeriness of the sound—like a soul temporarily separating from a body.

So there I was, standing there, getting a visual of something I could not possibly see. I wanted to just ignore what I knew. I didn't want to respond because I was afraid of what I would find. I didn't know if I could handle the blood and guts I was likely to see. I also knew that I have had the training to be a first responder. I felt morally obligated to go to this man's aid. As this internal argument continued, I felt compelled to assist, and began running down the street toward the accident. One side of my conscience was telling me I could turn back, that it wasn't too late- that no one had seen me or knew that I knew about the accident. The other side of my conscience urged me to hurry, that time was of the essence and that I would know what to do.

This internal battle continued, and as I rounded the corner of the main road I was first confronted by a little girl. Her mother, who was silent, was close by. The little girl's eyes instantly met mine and she said in an urgent calmness: "A man is hurt and he needs help." As I ran past the girl I told her that I knew and would help. She responded with: "Please help him. No one will help." I surveyed the scene and what first struck me were the people that were standing 50 feet or so from the vehicle. It was as if everyone was afraid to go any closer for fear of what they would find. There must have been four or five people standing and doing nothing. I continued to scan the scene and assessed that the SUV had made impact with a telephone pole, hit an Areca palm tree, then somehow rolled and landed upright on the side of the road. The telephone pole was a concern as it was bent at a 30° angle at the point of impact, and could come crashing down. Of more concern was the smoke coming from the car. I did not see or smell flames, but knew that was a potential. This was not a secure scene and the threat of danger was looming overhead. My attention now focused on the victim. Much to my amazement I saw a man sitting on the ground next to the driver side of his SUV. He was conscious. Not only was he conscious, but everything body-parts-wise was in its proper place. There was some minor blood splatter from an abrasion on his head; that was it.

By now I was about five feet from him and knew that I had an unstable scene with a male victim who was conscious and who had sustained a head injury. What I did not know was the extent of his injury or if there were any broken bones or internal injuries. What I instinctively knew was that the man was in shock and that he was going to lose consciousness. Time was of the essence, and my purpose became clear to me. I needed to get as much information as I could, before he lost consciousness.

"Sir, I am here to help you. Can you tell me your name." "Sir, what is your name?" He was disoriented and to complicate matters there was a language barrier. He said his name, but I did not understand. Fortunately, he understood me, so I continued with my questioning. "How did you end up on the ground, sir?" He replied: "I crawled out. I had to get out." This was a good sign, but did not mean he was not seriously injured. When faced with life or death, the human body is capable of incredible strength and can block awareness of pain that signals injury. It is a combination of shock and adrenalin that provides the opportunity to escape death; even if there is a life-threatening injury present. I continued my questioning, asking the man his age, if he was diabetic, what medications he was on, if he had a history of stroke or heart attack. He was becoming increasingly disoriented and irritable, and was having increasing difficulty responding to my questions. I knew he was going to lose consciousness within seconds. I asked if there was anyone he wanted us to contact. He was able to say his wife, stated the phone number, and then lost consciousness. How fortunate we are to live in an age of communication, for by now the bystanders had crept closer. 911 had already been called. As the man said the numbers for the phone number of his wife, the bystanders entered the number in their cell phones. I pointed at one of the responders with the cell phone and told him what to tell the wife—that her husband was in an accident, had been conscious and asking for her to be informed, and that EMS was on the way. I also told him to keep her on the line until law enforcement arrived.

I still had an unconscious man with undetermined injuries, a smoking SUV, and a telephone pole that was bent at a 30 degree angle. Another responder was looking at the SUV and did not appear concerned about the smoke. He did not announce himself or his credentials, but I saw the radio on his belt and knew he was probably off duty and in some sort of civil service. I was annoyed because he refused to answer me when I asked him to identify himself. It was a mute point, as law enforcement and EMS arrived within seconds. I advised the officer of the man with the cell phone who had the wife on the phone. Then I advised the ambulance crew of the information I had obtained from the driver of the vehicle. My role was over, and as quickly as I had stepped into a take-charge role, I quietly walked away and headed on back home.

I thought about how I had hesitated and had not wanted to respond. Just then the little girl reappeared, and again looking into my eyes she said: "Thank you for helping that man." She wanted to know if he was 'going to be alright' and I explained as best I could that he seemed to be and that he would be taken care of now. You know, it's funny. Not that I needed to be thanked, because that was not my motive or intention. But, of all the adults involved that day none said a word to me. None asked me any questions or commented on the incident. None thanked me. *It was the wisdom of a five year old little girl who voiced the need for help and then acknowledged with thanks.* In reality, the Good Samaritan that day was the little girl. It was her purist intent that taught the lesson. The lesson was about helping, even when it is frightening, because we are here to help one another. It was about gratitude for helping another soul. It was that simple. In fact, it was even simpler than that, because it was about love. Love and fear cannot coexist. This child did not exhibit any fear, only love. I felt the blessing of love from her that day, and was humbled by the lesson.

Interestingly, the little girl and her mother moved away seemingly days after that accident. It was as if our paths were meant to cross that one brief moment in time. It was yet another synchronistic moment in time that heightened my awareness of a Higher Order to the events in life.

*(The accident made the local paper the next day, and noted that the man lost control of his SUV because he had fire ants on his feet and had tried to brush them off. His SUV hit the telephone pole and flipped. He was treated at the hospital for a minor head injury and released.)*

## The Boy on Blood Mountain

In November, 2008, I was on vacation hiking with three other women in North Georgia. We donned ourselves the "Blue Ridge Girls," and as their leader I was determined to take them on as many trails as we could hike in a week's time. Blood Mountain is the highest peak on Georgia's portion of the Appalachian Trail, and is the state's sixth highest mountain. The origin of the name Blood Mountain is debated. Some believe that it was named after the color of the lichen and Catawba rhododendron growing near the rocky summit. Others believe that the name of the mountain comes from a bloody battle between the Cherokee and Creek Indians. Archaeological evidence has been discovered that tends to back the story of the battle, but the date of the battle and its participants are still hotly disputed due to the fact that there is only an oral history of the event. It is said that in the late 1600s, the Cherokee and Creek Indians began to compete for resources and fought a bloody battle on the mountain near Slaughter Gap. The Creek lost, ceding Blood Mountain to the Cherokee, who considered it a holy place.

On this particular day we were up by 5:30 a.m. and ready to take on one of my favorite trails on Blood Mountain. We headed up the Byron Herbert Reese Trail and reached Flat Rock Gap within 25 minutes. On our way, we heard two Pileated woodpeckers and also ruffed grouse. The grouse were drumming in what appeared to be either a demonstration concerning territory or a mating ritual. We did not see the grouse, yet heard them from across the valley. I also heard cardinals, blue jays, and ravens along the trail. Step after step, the freshly fallen leaves from the tree tops continued to rain on us, coloring our path with a palette of brilliant oranges, reds, and yellows.

The Appalachian Trail to Blood Mountain is without question my favorite trail, due to the fact that there is a good mix of level ground, switchbacks, and rock outcrops. It seems like 5 miles to the top of Blood Mountain, but in reality it is 1.5 miles. There are many stairways made from rock. The last leg of the trail is really exciting because you start to encounter more rock outcrops. Then you come upon a huge rock slab (the side of the mountain) that is all up hill. When we reached the top of this rock slab, I was awestruck by the scenery before me. Mountains looked like waves rolling in the distance. There were so many mountains I couldn't count them all. The sky was blue and there were a few cumulous clouds. The temperature was a perfect 70 degrees, and the sun was warm on my face. I felt on top of the world, yet humbled by the glory of a power far greater than me. We continued to ascend 2 more rock slabs before reaching the very top. We spent about an hour at the summit, sitting in quiet meditation, eating lunch, and resting up for our descent. There is a shelter that is built from rock, and it beckons the observer to think about the work that went into building the structure and how many have sought refuge over the years from the elements. This mountain exudes a strong spiritual/healing energy. I felt centered again, at one with the Tao. When we saw storm clouds approaching from the distance, we knew it was time to descend back down the trail.

Along the trail we passed many hikers who were on their way up the mountain. One group of hikers caught my immediate attention. There were two adult men and two young boys dressed in green, and wearing blazingly orange vests. One of the boys was frail, with pale skin. In fact, his face was so pale it was literally blue. It was clear to me that this was a sick child. He appeared to be only 9 or 10, yet death was hovering over him. A sense came over me that this child had leukemia and would not survive. I wondered how he had the strength and stamina to get this far up the mountain. Even better yet, I wondered why they were taking him on this excursion. The gear on their backs suggested their plan was to spend the night, despite the fact that a storm front was quickly moving in, brining rain and 40 degree temperatures.

I heard one of the men exclaim: "Wait, his shoe is untied." He helped the boy to a rock to sit on, and then began to tie the boy's shoe for him. I looked into the boys eyes and saw love and innocence looking back at me. I felt like I knew this soul—like we have known each other from the other side and will meet again. I had this sense that this boy was alive to be an example for others, to teach by example. Pure love and light emanated from his soul. He held out his staff (walking stick) to me. I asked him if he wanted me to hold it for him. He shook his head "no" and just smiled lovingly. Then he spoke in a humble, soft voice, inquiring: "Is there shelter?" I reassured him that there was shelter at the top, and that he would be dry and warm. With relief and a smile, he whispered "Oh good." Then the man helped the boy up and they started back up the mountain. I watched in awe, thinking this boy seemed more connected to Spirit than to the earth plane. I was humbled and moved to tears by this child. I was grateful to him for modeling fortitude, courage, humility, kindness, and love. I felt blessed by his presence that day. As part of the human experience, we tend to get bogged down with the complexities of life. As a general rule we put so much emphasis on our problems and all the things that are not going our way, and not enough energy into all that we have to be grateful for. We start to take things for granted, getting caught in the material items that bring us comfort and stimulation. The boy on the mountain reminded me that we are spiritual at our core. We are here on a journey, with an invitation to gain knowledge and wisdom, to connect to every living being, to grow and expand spiritually, in service to an all knowing, loving Source. At such a tender age, this boy was a model of living in the moment, in a state of gratitude. He raised the bar for me that day, encouraging me to complain less, be thankful more, and stay on the trail.

# CHAPTER FIVE

# HEALING

For as long as I can remember I have wanted to be a healer. As a child, when I was asked the age old question "what do you want to be when you grow up?" my response was: "a veterinarian." I have always had a connection with animals. The closest thing that I can compare it to is telepathy. I just seem to know what they are thinking and feeling and feel such a magnetic pull toward them. My spirit vibrates with joy when I am in the presence of an animal. As a veterinarian, I could "talk to the animals" and take care of them as well. The dream of being a vet became a fantasy the day my close friend Melinda advised me of three things: 1) there were only 7 vet schools in the country, 2) you had to be super bright just to get in because there was so much competition, and 3) it was really hard for females to get accepted to a vet school. At the time (the early 1970's) it was rare to encounter a female veterinarian. In fact, women had only just begun to break through the occupational barriers that had been in place throughout history. I clearly remember being in the school band and that my first, second, third choice of instruments was: drums, trombone, and trumpet. I was told that these were instruments that boys played. I was offered two choices, flute or clarinet, and neither appealed to me. I chose the clarinet, but my heart was never in it. If my elementary school system would not allow me to play 'boys instruments,' how was I to even dream about getting into a male dominated profession. My dream ended then and there.

What did not end was this inner drive to be part of healing. While in college I considered becoming an athletic trainer. The coursework I was taking would have put me within four credits of Pre-Med school. I was not confident in my intellectual abilities, and even though I wanted to a physician I did not dare to dream about that. However, a career in the medical field did seem possible, as I was learning that there were many trades within the profession. I became a certified Emergency Medical Technician. Despite the fact that I had the flu and was running a fever on the day of my exam, I scored out within the top 3% of all the students who took the exam in the State of New York. This was significant for me because it proved to me that I was not stupid (as I believed I was) and that I now had the knowledge and skills to be the healer/helper that I always wanted to be. There was just this little problem that got in the way.

I may have acquired the knowledge and skills to be in the medical field, however, when "in the field" I kept feeling like I was going to faint. I was told that once I became desensitized I would not feel faint anymore. It didn't seem to matter what I was seeing that was causing me to feel faint. During my intern in the ER, I was observing a physician suture a little boy's knee. This was really no big deal, in the sense that there was not a lot of blood, there was no big wound—just a small cut that needed maybe four or five sutures. As soon as I started to see the black dots before my eyes I left the room. Another time in the ER, the physician was very excited for me because I was going to be able to observe a thorocentesis. This was to be performed on an elderly woman. The procedure requires puncturing a hole from the back into the lung in order to drain fluid and relieve pressure. As soon as the elderly woman groaned the black spots appeared before my eyes and, again, I was out of the room. Each time I got out of the room just before I passed out. I was encouraged to continue on and assured that the fainting sensation would eventually go away.

My final answer on my career in the medical profession came one day when I was working in a youth runaway shelter. There was an 18 year old male who had been treated days prior, for a fractured nose. He came to me and asked me to help him change the packing that was in his nose. This was truly no big deal. He was not in any pain and I even questioned why he needed help. We went into the bathroom and I don't even think we got very far. I probably just looked at his nose and saw those damn black dots. Before I knew it the walls of the room started closing in on me and I started to feel that spinning sensation. I was determined not to faint over something so silly. I tried to shake it off and continue—only to find that the room was spinning to such a degree that I was losing my balance. I was not only losing my balance, I was losing the battle. It was as if I had been in the boxing ring and had just taken a sucker punch. I was headed for the canvas. Only problem was that I was not in a boxing ring. I was in a very small bathroom. What I hit face first, was not the canvas, but the bathroom sink.

There are some universal signs in this world. One is the universal sign of choking. That's when someone who is choking grabs their throat with both hands. Well, the universal sign of a broken nose is when someone grabs their nose with both hands—which is exactly what I did after my face crashed into the bathroom sink. Ok, so now I'm in the process of fainting, which was interrupted by my face slamming into the sink, and now I have a bigger problem because I'm going to pass out from head trauma---all over changing the bandages on someone else's nose. Well, I'm a little like Rocky Balboa. I was not going down. I was determined to shake this off. The poor guy that I was "helping" was beside himself with concern. I kept hearing him say "Are you ok? Are you ok?" In my stupor, I could hear myself saying: "Yeah, I'm fine. I just need to walk this off."

That seemed to be the answer to me. Walk this off. Don't give in. Just 'mind over matter' this 'passing out moment'. You're ok. So, I opened the bathroom door and decided to walk down the hall to my office. Yeah, that was the answer. Walk to my office and shake it off. As I made my way down the blurry hall, I continued to hear this kid quietly saying: "Are you ok? Are you sure you are ok?" As much as I was trying to assure him that I was just fine, I was finding it more and more necessary to focus on my goal of getting to my office so that I could sit in my chair. Well, the Rocky Balboa in me managed to get to my chair—where I then proceeded to pass out.

From a far away distance I could hear the nurse yelling my name. When I came around she told me that it 'took a while' to get me back and she was just about to call 911. By now it was obvious that I wasn't "fine," yet I assured her that 911 really wasn't necessary. The next day I saw my physician, who confirmed that I not only fractured my nose, but had a really nice concussion on top of that. I experienced a real banger of a headache for the next two weeks, along with some mental confusion. It was at that point that I realized that there was not going to be any 'mind over matter' for me with this issue. In fact, this little fainting issue was not going to go away. It was time to accept that, while I may have the intelligence, knowledge, and skills to be in the medical profession—this was not my purpose on this earth plane. My career as an EMT was officially over.

Yet there was still this feeling deep within that I was on this earth plane to be a healer. Sometimes I feel "it" in my hands. Other times it is what I seem to inherently "know." I am by no means a medical intuitive, and yet I have had experiences where I knew seemingly more than I should. One example of this occurred while I was an adjunct instructor teaching at a community college. I was teaching an evening class and working off the whiteboard, about five or ten minutes into my lesson, when I suddenly had some urgent information about a student. The information was telepathic in nature, and coming from one of my Spirit Guides. I was overwhelmed with a sense of urgency, and as I began to tell my Spirit Guide that I was 'in the middle of something' I had a physical compulsion within my soul to immediately interrupt what I was doing. Can you imagine sitting in a college class and having the instructor stop in mid-sentence loudly proclaiming: **"Oh, alright!"** I put my dry erase marker down, turned to one of my students and said: "I am not a doctor. I have no empirical evidence based on what I am about to tell you. However, I am getting a message that something is very seriously wrong with you and that it is urgent that you see your doctor. Please promise me that you will call your doctor in the morning and make an immediate appointment. I don't know what's wrong, other than it seems like it is not in a specific location but within your entire system. I don't mean to frighten you, but I feel an obligation to let you know you must see your physician immediately." Then I apologized for the interruption and went back to my lesson. It mattered not what any of my students thought, and I quickly dismissed the fact that whole event had even taken place.

The following week, when the class met again, the student announced to the class that she had followed my request and was seen by her physician the next day. Her physician had some blood tests performed and she was told that her system was being poisoned by something in her home. She had been feeling weak and fatigued, but did not know how sick she was. Her physician stated that had she not made the appointment, she would have been dead within 48 hours. She was immediately ordered to evacuate her home, and was now experiencing an alleviation of her symptoms.

Another time that I "knew" was when I was working at a residential chemical dependence treatment center. One of my jobs was to provide approval for clients seeking admission to the program. A white male, 30-40 years old, had requested admission. John was an alcoholic, and he had cirrhosis. The cirrhosis was so advanced that he was given six months to live. He was incontinent (wearing diapers) and jaundiced (yellow in appearance). From the paperwork alone, I knew this man was not appropriate for our program. He needed a hospice program, not a residential program that required 18 hours of full participation each day. I declined his request.

John did not accept my decision, and almost every day he would come to the site to ask us to reconsider. I knew this because I would see the car drive up (his father drove him) and then I would watch as the passenger side door would slowly open and this gravely ill man would take small staccato steps to the admissions office. The distance from the parking lot to the admissions office would normally take a healthy person less than two minutes. It took him about ten minutes. He was yellow, with a distended abdomen (ascites) and moved in a painfully slow manner. The admissions counselor kept appealing to me to admit this man, stating that his dying wish was to be admitted to our program so that he could die sober. She showed me the paperwork from the physician's office saying that John had six months to live. I countered, saying that he would not make it two months. When I was asked how I knew that, all I could say was "I just know."

Well, John would just not take no for an answer, and he came to the admissions office almost every day for a month. He was breaking my heart. I've never seen anyone literally dying to get in to a residential program. He was no longer drinking, just dying, yet desperately wanting to be a part of something that represented life. I met with my administration and explained the risks. Those risks included sudden deterioration and even death. I met with the clients and explained the risks. It was imperative for them to understand that being around this man was going to be unpleasant. For one, when someone is dying of cirrhosis there is a very unpleasant odor that comes from the pores of the skin. Jaundice can be so severe that it is distressing, even nauseating to look at. Mental confusion is very common, due to the high level of toxins circulating within the body. At the worst, this man could literally die in his sleep in the dormitory where the men slept. I also explained that coming into our program was this man's dying wish. The group considered this an honor, and the unanimous decision was that he should be admitted to the program.

This whole process took about a month, and I knew that death was now imminent. Despite this, the call was made and we admitted our alcoholic friend to the program. The dying have much to teach about life, and so it was with John. He was not disruptive, despite the fact that he was physically in pain and nearly incapacitated by his illness. He would share appropriately and profoundly during groups, causing awe amongst the rest of the client population. He spoke to the will to live and the opportunities that they all still had, if they but made the decision to maintain sobriety one day at a time. His presence on the unit was a gift. Not one client complained. Indeed, there was an air of quiet gratitude. I received a call from my evening staff of the seventh day of his admission. John had apparently gone to staff and clients alike to announce that his body was "shutting down" (his words) and that it was time for him to leave. Alcoholics are notoriously selfish during active illness and even well into early recovery. Yet this man, despite how compromised he was, was selfless enough to remove himself from the very thing he so desperately wanted in order to not upset the treatment community. John went home that night and died within a day or two. Despite tears for the man and what he could have been, we rejoiced in what he modeled for us in his final living moments. In the end, he received what he so desperately wanted—he died sober. We were the better for having had the privilege of knowing him.

Sometimes there is a peace in knowing. Sometimes it is better to do the ethically/spiritually/intuitively "right" thing than the clinically appropriate thing. This man taught me to listen with my heart and not just my brain. He taught me that sometimes taking a risk can be wiser than doing the smart thing by playing it safe. Ultimately, he taught me a little more about this thing called Love.

So, in my desire as a child to be a healer, I have now arrived as an adult with two questions: 1) what is a healer? 2) who is the healer? I thought a healer worked with the flesh, and so my original quest was to be in the medical field. Having discovered that the medical field is not my calling, I turned my focus toward healing the mind. In the process, I find that healing is just as much spiritual as it is mental or physical. What I have observed is that a "healer" can only assist in the healing process of those who want to be healed. In the counseling profession there are so many who need and ask for help, yet they continue to exhibit symptoms of illness despite receiving help. Healing requires change, action, internalization, responsibility, honesty, willingness, courage, and perseverance. One who does not practice these qualities will surely return to illness—even if healed.

So, even if I can assist a person in a process of change, does that make me a healer? I've come to believe that no one entity can take the credit, because there is a trinity that exists between God, the being that is needing healing, and the one facilitating the process ("the healer"). All three have an integral part in this process. Actually, the healer acts more as a conduit for change. The power to heal comes through Spirit and must be embraced by the receiver. A healer is a conduit, who fosters change. If that is true, then the person needing healing can also be the healer. Truth be told, I have probably learned far more from those that I have worked with than they from me. Those that I have come in contact with have taught me so much about life and given me many spiritual gifts. In the process they have been an integral part of my healing journey.

*Part 2:*

# GIFTS FROM GOD'S CREATURES

# CHAPTER ONE

# IN GOD'S TIME

There have been many companion animals in my life, each having a special place in my heart. All have been either rescue animals or adopted from shelters. Each provided me with a precious gift, and in return I tried to provide a safe, secure home with abundant food and love. I believe that the animals of the planet are the custodians of the earth. I have nothing but respect for every creature that inhabits this planet. Our domestic companions may more adequately be described as companions of our souls—if we but let them. They ask for so little, and give so much in return.

One of my cherished companions was Bijou. Bijou was being highlighted at the Humane Society because he had been there a long time. He was a lab mix and was seven years old. It's tough to compete with a cute cuddly puppy when you are in your senior years. Week after week people walked by Bijou's cage, not even giving him a glance. I had the adoption counselor bring him into an acquaintance room so that we could meet. There was something special about this dog. I have to admit, though, that I was concerned about his age. I wasn't sure what the life expectancy of a lab was, but I figured he probably had another two-four years. He was full of life and seemed to be begging for the chance for a new home. The adoption counselor noted that he was fully housebroken, was leash trained and socialized to other pets. Bijou had a way of communicating with me telepathically. It was as if there was an instant bond. We understood one another. He did not want to die at the shelter, and I was not about to let him. The papers were signed and Bijou left the doors of the Humane Society with tail wagging.

An animal behavioralist once told me that newly adopted companion animals are always on their best behavior the first couple of weeks. After that period of time their "true nature" comes out and you begin to see their "bad" behaviors. Bijou settled in pretty quickly and appeared to be on his best behavior. He was well-mannered, and never barked. While he was not a behavior problem at all, he was not the best at commands (like "sit," "lay down," and "come"). He also appeared to have some separation anxiety, as he did not leave my side. In fact he was never out of my sight. It was now three weeks since the adoption, and Bijou still hadn't barked. I began to wonder why and if this was perhaps a trait of his breed.

Bijou came to work with me every day. He was well behaved, had a calming presence, and seemed to be a natural at being a therapy dog for the clients. One day Bijou started walking out the door of my office, which was uncharacteristic of him. I called for him and he did not come. I lowered my tone and raised the volume, and still no response. I joking said out loud: "What are you deaf!!" And then it hit me, as I exclaimed: "Oh my God, he's deaf." I got up out of my chair, walked directly behind him, and started snapping my fingers right behind his ears. No response. I began clapping my hands. Not even a flinch. I yelled out his name. Nothing. Bijou was deaf! He was 100%, totally, completely, deaf. I was stunned. I had this dog for three weeks and didn't know he was deaf. He had been at the Humane Society for over a month and no one picked up on the fact that he was deaf (I knew the staff. They were well trained and would have reported it if they had picked up on it.). I began to wonder if his previous owner had known. There was no history, no way to know. Now I understood why he never barked, as he could not hear anything to bark at!

I had to communicate with Bijou that I knew he was deaf. I wanted to break through the isolation that he had existed in. I had learned sign language when I worked for the county. I took classes for a year and became good enough to communicate with a maintenance worker who was deaf. I never expected to use this skill with an animal. Verbal commands ceased and I began to communicate with eye contact and hand signals. Bijou seemed to know almost instantly that I understood. It was as if he was rejoicing that someone finally understood that he could not hear. He learned signs for "sit," "come," "walk," "good," "love," and the sign for applause. Bijou no longer had to follow me from room to room. He understood that if I needed him I would walk up to him and give him the sign for come. He became more relaxed and less vigilant. He was so grateful to be understood and so eager to please. We were a perfect partnership.

A per diem staff member came in one day to facilitate an education group. She was of French heritage. She was a favorite among the clients because she taught with enthusiasm and had the gift of making learning fun. She loved dogs and connected with Bijou immediately, saying with glee: "Bijou!! Do you know what that means?" I am 'culturally challenged' and honestly hadn't recognized Bijou as being a French word. She told me that Bijou meant "magnificent gem." I was so impressed with the accuracy of this given name, for this dog was truly a magnificent gem. It was the perfect name because it so aptly described him. It was poetic and grand, and so was Bijou. Every day spent with Bijou was a gift and a joy. There was not one day that I did not feel total gratitude at his presence in my life. Being with Bijou was effortless. There was rarely a time when we were apart.

Then, one night I was awakened at 3:00am to the sound of Bijou coughing violently. It was as if he could not get enough air. He was clearly in distress and I rushed him to the Emergency Vet. The vet took X-Rays and came into the room with news that I was not prepared for. Bijou had cancer in 90% of his lungs. The vet did not know how he had survived to that point with no signs of distress, or how he had lived this long. There was absolutely nothing that could be done. The vet gave me the option of spending a few quality hours with Bijou and then taking him to my own vet to be euthanized. I was beside myself with grief. I took Bijou home, and later that morning took Bijou to my vet. I had Bijou for only 9 months. It seemed a cruel fate for both of us to have found one another only to be ripped apart after only 9 months. I loved him heart and soul and knew he felt the same about me. My vet was just as stunned, as she had seen no indications of respiratory distress and never would have even suspected lung cancer. Just like his deafness, Bijou had managed to quietly suffer without any one even suspecting that something was wrong. Only now, he could hardly breathe, and he needed to be relieved of his suffering. I sat on the floor with Bijou and he put his head in my lap. He was ready, and wanted to be near me in passing. The vet was incredibly compassionate. She was visibly moved by the process that was unfolding and throughout the euthanasia she kept whispering: "I'm sorry. I'm so sorry. I'm sorry." Quiet tears slipped down my cheeks and for the first time in nine months I communicated a spoken work to Bijou. "Send me the next one, Bijou. Send me a light for my heart." Bijou passed quietly. I was racked with grief. My only consolation was that I had provided him with a loving home from which to cross over. Bijou was cherished and he knew that. I am so blessed to have been given the opportunity to provide him with that gift.

I am not one to want to rush out and obtain another pet when one crosses over. I understand why some do, and don't hold judgment. I personally, usually need time to grieve before I can freely extend myself to a new companion. When I lost Bijou I felt differently. My heart was so broken and there was such a void in my world that I think I started the search for a companion within a week. Always partial to Dobermans and Danes, I decided to search the Doberman Rescue website. There was a young female Doberman that was in a foster home full of other Dobies. I figured that if not her, I'd want one of the others.

It was a 2 ½ hour drive to get to the Doberman foster home. There were about six rescue Dobies in this house. Nova was a nine month old who had somehow failed to complete the training program to become a Search and Rescue dog. Having failed her training, she was sent to Doberman Rescue for adoption. She came with papers, which meant nothing in terms of her value because she was spayed and could not reproduce. At nine months of age, Nova would have been born the same month that I had adopted Bijou. I liked the name Nova, and only knew that there was a science show on PBS called Nova. I didn't need a lot of time with her to decide she was coming home with me. She had an incredibly soft disposition that exuded love. She was a mess from living in a foster home—full of ticks and fleas—but nothing a bath and patient grooming couldn't fix. When I got home I looked up the word "Nova" in the dictionary. It means "a bright shining star." How fitting (and synchronistic), for my 'magnificent gem' sent me a 'bright shining star.' Indeed, Nova is a light in my heart. She is my bright shining star full of the white light of the Holy Spirit. She is love to her very core. The synchronicity of this sequence of events coming "full circle" has been a comfort to me.

Nova is now ten years of age at this writing. For many years I wondered why she didn't complete the academy to become a Search and Rescue dog. When I adopted her she was a 'little soldier.' She had obviously received a militaristic training and was clearly conditioned to be a working dog. At nine months of age, Nova did not know what play was. She did not truly know what love was. She had plenty to offer, but had not been given much in return. Play and love were foreign to her. She was so militarized that she would refuse food and water throughout the 'working day.' She was a super obedient little soldier. My colleagues at work were swift to put a stop to that. Despite my "no human food" rule, I would frequently find my colleagues smuggling special treats in to Nova. One day, I returned to my office from an assessment I had completed to find Nova sitting on a chair with a Nurse spoon-feeding her soup! The nurse lit up when she saw me and exclaimed: "She likes it!" What was not to like? Nova was pampered and loved and played with and quickly outgrew the regimented lifestyle she had been born into. Today, Nova is an indoor dog, who prefers the comfort of a couch and air conditioning.

It took years, but I finally put the puzzle together. Having been certified as an Emergency Medical Technician I knew what seizures were. I was convinced that Nova was having seizures periodically. I consulted with my veterinarian and learned that epilepsy is not uncommon in Dobermans. I believe that Nova was rejected as a working dog because she has epilepsy. She most likely had seizures and was brought to Doberman Rescue. Her condition was probably not disclosed for fear that she would not be accepted or adopted out. In fact, Nova's seizures typically occur when she is sleeping and can be very subtle. An untrained eye may have never even noticed. So, talk about 'full circle…' My disabled dog, my magnificent gem, which I was honored to spend nine months with, sent me a disabled dog, a bright shining star for my heart, which was born at the time Bijou came into my life (making her nine months old when she came home with me). Now that is synchronicity at its best, in God's time.

# CHAPTER TWO

# THE GIFT OF GLORY

## _The Hole_

At one time in my life I was fortunate enough to live on the beach. My partner and I were renting a tiny little apartment that was in Hollywood, Fl. The apartment was on a street hardly used by vehicles, and the beach was just 15 steps from the front door. I literally watched the sun rise up over the ocean every day. What a joy to be able to experience such beauty. The ocean exuded a vibration that generated a solace within the depths of my soul that breathed a constant sensation of renewal. This was a healing place.

One of our passions was scuba diving, and shortly after moving into this beachside apartment we decided to do a beach dive. This activity required caution and some vigilance, as we did not have a boat to protect us from other boaters, nor did we have anyone around to assist with navigation. We were essentially traveling into an area where neither had 'gone before.' The other issue with regard to a beach dive is that it requires swimming out to sea to a depth where one can actually scuba dive. The Florida coast can be very shallow for quite some time before it drops down in depth. We had no way of knowing how long we would have to swim out before we could get to even 30 feet of water. We also had no way of knowing if it would be worth it, as there was no way of knowing what we would find. We had been diving in some of the best places in the Florida Keys, and here we were doing a trivial little beach dive off of Hollywood Florida.

It was a warm, sunny summer morning. The ocean was nearly flat, which was perfect for this kind of dive. Even better was that the visibility was very good. We snorkeled out to sea, with scuba gear on, for what felt like an eternity. The landscape of the ocean floor was barren. For what seemed like a ¼ mile all one could see was sand and an occasional shell. I was beginning to think that this was all a big mistake, as there was hardly any life form to be found. Then, seemingly out of nowhere was a small French Grunt fish. It just started swimming alongside us, and then slightly ahead. We followed, and soon another one joined us. At first, I thought these two fish were cute and I was mildly entertained because the barren sand had started to bore me. As we swam further out to sea it began to occur to me that these two fish were not following us, they were leading us. We got to a depth that required scuba gear and descended. Our fish friends were waiting, and our escort continued. The landscape began to change and soon Porkfish joined our escort. As the landscape transformed from sand to coral reef, Atlantic Spadefish and Gray Angelfish arrived on the scene. The Gray Angelfish were the largest I had ever seen—about 2 feet. I was awestruck at the size of the Spadefish and Gray Angelfish, and even more awestruck at how friendly they were. There were so many of them (at least a dozen of each) in this concentrated area, and they seemed to be welcoming us in glorious fashion.

Then, seemingly out of nowhere, we came upon a hole in the ocean floor that was like a glorious reef-city. It was full of hundreds of tropical fish in what appeared to be a harmonious, utopia-like existence. Every kind of tropical fish that I had ever seen on all my dives combined, was now all in one place. Blue Parrotfish, Queen Parrotfish, French Angelfish, Queen Angelfish, Gray Angelfish, Atlantic Spadefish, Porkfish, Triggerfish, Squirrelfish, Spanish Hogfish, Rock Beauty, Sergeant Majors, Yellowhead Wrasse, Puffers, Purple Wrasse. I have never seen so many different kinds of fish in such a concentrated area. The other phenomenal thing was that these fish were all large and brilliant in color. The greatest gift was that they were not afraid of humans. They greeted us. They swam up against me and wove in and out of my hands in a welcoming gesture that was beyond anything I had ever experienced. Strange as it may seem, these fish were interacting with me in a telepathic welcome that was undeniable. I was in an underwater heaven. Everywhere I looked was a glorious testament to the perfect work of God. It was as if this sacred place was untouched by man. It was a small area that was surrounded by that barren sand I was talking about—as if nothing else was around for miles.

I continued to explore the rocks and crevices. This hole was teaming with lobster. I had never seen so many lobsters in one area. Most would think of dinner at a time like this—as it was free for the taking. But that was not my purpose, and I would never have even dreamed of disturbing such a beautiful place. I was a guest in their home, and they had welcomed me with glorious fanfare. I saw the lobster tentacles and began to touch them lightly with my fingertips. To my joy, they touched back. We engaged in a dance, the tentacles and I, and slowly the lobster emerged from the crevice. We were brailing one another in an exchange of genuine love. There was no fear. This lobster had no fear of me, just curiosity and peace. I thanked him, and went on to the next pair of tentacles and the same thing occurred. I was interacting with lobsters! We were dancing with a sensory exchange of peace and harmony.

All around me was peace and love and beauty. I was in a very special place that perhaps few others had visited. It was not tainted by man. It was pure. I felt an extreme honor and glowed with gratitude for all the sea-dwelling creatures of this underwater city. I would have stayed forever, if not for the time-limit that my scuba tank provided. It was time to make the long swim back. We were escorted back in much the same manner. A small group of fish took us part of the way, which then parted, and then two fish took us the rest of the way. My dive partner and I decided this would be our personal secret, as we did not want this to be ruined by frequent human visitation. We went on this dive a few more times, and each time the same process would unfold. We would be met by a small French Grunt, which would be joined by Porkfish, which would escort us to The Hole, where we would initially be welcomed by huge Atlantic Spadefish and Gray Angelfish. We never had to worry about how to find The Hole. We were taken to it. It is a memory that is indelibly etched in my memory, one that is as real today as it was the first time I visited.

By the way, after that dive I was never able to eat lobster again. Nor am I likely to even eat fish. I know that sounds a bit extreme, but it would be like eating a kindred spirit. For now, I just can't do it. I'll survive if I never eat lobster again. The experience was just that powerful. It was a gift from the ocean that was as humbling as it was beautiful. I witnessed a harmony that words cannot describe. All was in balance, there was no fear. It was a gift of Grace, a blessed place that exuded Love. It was also a reminder to respect and be humbled by a glorious power that is far greater than me.

## Bugs

It was a cool early morning. I was sitting in the parking lot of Home Depot, in my brother's work truck, waiting for him to return. He had not disclosed what he was going in to buy or even what was on the agenda for the day. The quiet of morning has always been a distinct pleasure for me. I enjoy watching the birds and squirrels begin their day and, as such, did not mind having a few meditative moments to myself. My brother got into the truck and put his Home Depot purchase on the seat. "Bugs." he said. I waited for more information, and when nothing else was forthcoming I said: "Bugs? What bugs? What are we doing?" He indicated that the herb garden that we had planted for a woman who lived on the beach was now apparently full of bugs and she wanted us to exterminate them. I found it a bit odd that we were now responsible for maintaining the herb garden, and wondered why this woman even wanted an herb garden if she wasn't actually doing the gardening herself. I reminded myself that this was the very same woman who watched us plant four palm trees in the Florida summer swelter (in the middle of August, during a drought), literally on the beach (trying to dig a four foot hole in dry sand is quite a challenge), and then after we were all done told my brother that one of the trees "needed to be moved six inches." I was not amused by this woman, or her privileged attitude.

The herb garden had mostly parsley, dill, oregano, and basil. I was pleased with how large the plants had grown. My brother and I had spent an entire day building this garden, and now I was seeing how productive our labor was. We kneeled by the plants to see what kind of "bugs" we were about to kill. I was expecting to find tiny insects and there were none. The plants were all very healthy. What we found were caterpillars. My brother announced that it was going to be a shame to kill them. I was pleased that he had some compassion, yet irritated that he didn't see the obvious solution. I exclaimed: "Kill them! Hell no, we're not going to kill them. I'll pick every single one of them off and then you can spray the plants." He thought this was very silly, yet he decided to humor me and allow me the time needed to remove the caterpillars. I ran to the truck and emptied my cooler to act as a make-shift home for the caterpillars. I clipped some parsley and placed that in the cooler for them to munch on while we went about our day. There were some 39 caterpillars. My brother really thought I was nuts when he saw me placing them in the cooler. He said "What are you going to do with them? You're crazy. Just let them go in the woods." I advised him that these caterpillars would likely die in the woods, as they were eating herbs—not regular leaves off the plants and trees. I told him that I was going to take them home and research them on the computer to find out what they were.

I tended to the caterpillars for the rest of the day, which was not easy as I couldn't keep the lid closed all day because they needed air. They were very active and it was difficult to keep them contained, and not squish them when opening and closing the cooler. By the end of the day there was only one casualty. Upon arriving home I placed them carefully in a fish tank that had a screen lid. I bought a bunch of parsley and lined the tank with it, and also put some dry twigs in the tank for them to climb on. My research on the computer indicated that the caterpillars were going to turn into Black Swallowtail Butterflies. I was so excited to be a part of what had turned out to be a rescue mission.

The caterpillars continued to thrive in my tank, eating fresh parsley from the grocery store every day. Days went by before I noticed that one of the caterpillars had turned into a chrysalis. It was brown, and attached to one of the twigs in the tank. It looked very small and rather unobtrusive and I wondered how this dried out looking thing was actually going to turn into a butterfly. With each passing day there were a few more chrysalises attached to the twigs or to the tank. This whole process took about a week, and then before I knew it there was no need to buy parsley anymore as the tank was full of 38 chrysalises. It takes approximately 10-14 days for the transformation from chrysalis to Black Swallowtail Butterfly to occur.

One morning I went out to check on the tank and found a newly hatched butterfly drying from the twig.

Butterflies when newly hatched are all wet and literally drip dry before they can take off into the world. They initially just hang there and then eventually start to slowly fan their wings. As they dry out even more they flutter about and then rest for a few minutes before testing their wing strength again. At this stage they are not afraid of humans. In fact, they will comfortably rest on your hand or clothing as they bask in the warmth of the sun. Each day, as a new set of butterflies would emerge I would take them from the tank and place them on nearby hibiscus plants to dry. With camera in hand I documented the transformation as it unfolded. I felt such gratitude and sheer joy at being a part of such a precious and glorious event.

You can call me crazy. I am ok with being crazy, even if it means going out of my way during a work day to defend the existence of a caterpillar; being inconvenienced by sacrificing my lunch cooler and tending to caterpillars; and making daily special trips to the grocery store to buy fresh parsley. I'm ok with standing up for nature and recognizing when a "bug" is one of the most fragile winged creatures that we have on this earth. I don't think I'm so crazy to see a foreshadow of transcendence. I don't think I'm so crazy to appreciate nature enough to assist it, especially when it is man's whims that are interfering with the natural order of things. No, I consider myself blessed to have been able to assist and allow such a glorious creature to thrive. I wish others would stop and take the time to see that there are options, that there is enough time and room for us to coexist with nature. I wish that more of us could see that the animals of this planet are the custodians of the earth and that without them we will cease to exist. We should be thanking the bugs on a daily basis for doing their part in this world, as God intended them to do. They are doing a good job. We, as a collective human species, are not.

What a glorious gift to have witnessed the transformation of 38 chrysalises. I was able to interact with these wonderful creatures, witness their beautiful colors, appreciate their delicate nature, and admire the intrinsic strength that will allow them to function in the elements of nature. What a glorious gift, and all thanks to the lady beachside who wanted those bugs exterminated.

# CHAPTER THREE

# THE GIFT OF CHARITY: MAKING ROOM FOR ONE MORE

*Of the many animals that I have acquired over the years, most of them have found their way to me via conventional means such as animal shelters or rescue leagues. However, there are other ways to wander into my heart. All it takes is the need for a home and a Higher Order to synchronize life events. Regardless of how they found their way to me, all of my companion pets have been cherished and have provided an abundance of joy, gratitude and love.*

## Sara

My brother lives in a rural part of town where it is common to find citrus groves, horses, and small farms. He lives on a 10 acre parcel of property where he owns a shop and runs his landscaping and lawn maintenance business. Between agency jobs I was fortunate enough to obtain employment as a laborer with my brother. It was demanding work that always got me in the best shape of my life. There's nothing like 8-11 hours of manual labor to convert fat to muscle. The days were long, dirty, and back breaking. I was grateful for the job and enjoyed the physical challenges the job always provided—despite the pain of it all.

I was not the newest worker on the job. The neighbor across the street had a farm and an irrigation business that was not reputable. Apparently, this neighbor had a need to leave the country quickly, and as a result he essentially abandoned his workers and most of his animals. The workers wandered over to my brother's property looking for a job. There were some 37 cats that were also on that property, along with goats, donkeys, and chickens. Most were relocated prior to the neighbor's disappearance. There was this one young cat who wandered over to my brother's property with the workers. She couldn't have been much over a year old. She was white, with tiger markings and was very friendly. Actually, she appeared to be more hungry than friendly. Each morning my brother would bring a Ziploc bag full of cat food from his house. This little cat would be waiting for the food each morning and would devour the portion my brother would give her. My brother would tuck the bag away to save for later in the day, or the next day. The workers knew a little about this cat's history and said that the neighbor across the street did not believe in feeding cats—that he believed that cats should catch and eat the mice on the farm. The only problem with that thinking, according to the workers, was that with 37 cats on the property there were not many mice. This cat was always in a constant search for food. No wonder she had wandered over to my brother's property—there simply wasn't enough food to survive across the street.

My brother quickly tired of this little cat's appetite. One morning he complained bitterly, as the cat was now "stealing" food from the baggie after she ate the food he had given her. He thought she was greedy. I explained to my brother that this little cat was stealing food because she needed the nourishment. She wasn't quite showing yet, but somehow I just knew she was pregnant. I thought that if my brother knew this he would be more compassionate and let her have whatever she wanted. To my disgust, my brother responded: "Is that why she's eating so much?! Well then, I'm not going to feed her any more. I don't want kittens. She'll have to move on." He meant it. Knowing my brother as I do, I knew there was no point in having a discussion about this. His mind was made up, and he would no longer care for this little being.

My heart went out to this little cat. She had such a tough start in life. It was just so sad that she finally found a food source, only to be cast away because she was pregnant. I knew that I had to intervene and help this cat. I had five cats of my own and just couldn't take yet another one in (let alone the kittens). Taking her to an animal shelter would likely mean euthanasia due to her pregnant condition, and that hardly seemed fair given her history. I decided to take her home and keep her in my garage until she came to term and delivered her kittens. At the end of my shift I put her in a crate and took her home with me.

The garage was not really a home, but I comforted myself with the fact that it was shelter from the elements. Having now taken care of basic needs like food and shelter, I next turned my attention to what to call this little one. She was deserving of a pretty name, something that would bring dignity to the life she had been born into. "Sara" came to mind as fitting, and she seemed to take to the name with ease and grace. Before I left her to explore her new environment, I sat down with Sara and explained the arrangement. She listened intently as I explained to her that this was not her new home. I told her that I had a house full and could not adopt her. I told her that I would take care of her, make sure she had plenty of food, and that I would see her through her pregnancy. I also promised that I would find good homes for her and all of her kittens. She seemed accepting of the arrangements, and proceeded to explore the confines of the garage.

Sara was barely showing when I took her in, and it was weeks before she was obviously pregnant. She was a grateful guest, never showing any interest to leave the garage. She seemed to be a very sweet, quiet cat. The only problem that I encountered was extreme mood swings. While I had bottle-fed many orphaned kittens, I had never been around a pregnant animal. All of my pets had been spayed or neutered. Sara's personality appeared to be heavily influenced by hormones. She would be all affection one minute, and would turn around and charge at you with incredulous hostility the next. It would have been comical had it not been so frightening. As she came closer to term her mood swings became even more pronounced. She would rub up against me in complete affection, but the minute I would get up to leave the garage, this cat would charge me with teeth exposed and nails extended. She was a psycho kitty!! I began to carry a pillow for protection whenever I entered the garage. Psycho Kitty was completely out of control. I was going on instinct, assuming it was hormones. It had to be, given the extremes of mood that I was witnessing.

Sara's belly got so big she looked like she would burst. When she grew increasingly restless and fidgety, I prepared a birthing box for her. I had learned from the workers that Sara had at least one, and possibly two previous pregnancies. The workers said that they never saw any of her kittens, and I assumed that she had either had a miscarriage or that the kittens had died shortly after birth. Given Sara's tender age and her malnutrition it would make sense that a previous pregnancy would not have been successful. Another week went by and Sara became increasingly uncomfortable. She seemed to appreciate the birthing box for its intended purpose, as she would periodically go in the box as if preparing for "the moment." I think I was as nervous as Sara, as this was my first pregnancy and I wasn't exactly sure what my role was going to be. I was excited about the opportunity to watch the birthing process, and hopeful that Sara would indulge me. I kept thinking the moment had arrived, only to find that yet another day would pass without kittens being born. Then, early one morning, I went out to check on Sara and found her in her birthing box with a tiny new born kitten. The kitten was not quite dry yet, and had tiger striped markings. The process had begun, and Sara was getting ready to birth her next kitten!!

Sara required absolutely no assistance from me. She seemed to appreciate my presence and support, and allowed me to witness the miracle of birth. As soon as a kitten would be born she would take care of the afterbirth (placenta, umbilical cord) and would lick her new born kitten clean. Having completed this, it seemed the next kitten would be ready for birthing. The timing was precise and perfect. There was most certainly a Higher Order to what I was observing. I watched in awe as Sara gave birth to three kittens, making a total of four. It was fun to watch the kittens dry, as it was not until then that you could discern what the kitten actually looked like. The first born was tiger- striped; the second had the color markings of a Siamese seal-point, the third and fourth were black and white.

Sara had given birth to four healthy kittens. There was just one problem. Once Sara had finished giving birth and cleaning them up, she left the birthing box and seemed to have absolutely no interest in her kittens. At first I thought that maybe she just needed a break from the delivery, that this was nature's way of regaining strength. However, I became increasingly concerned because Sara was not attending to the kittens at all. She was not feeding them and did not appear protective of them. In fact, Sara was showing no interest in her babies at all. I was convinced now that Sara did have previous pregnancies and that her kittens had been still born. As far as Sara was concerned her job was over. She was practiced at giving birth, but new nothing of motherhood. I tried placing the kittens at Sara's nipples, but Sara would just get up and go sit away from the kittens. She was refusing to nurse her kittens.

It was time now for me to intervene. The kittens would quickly die if they were not nourished. The problem is that the probability of them surviving was very poor, even if I bottle fed them. Newborns require a mother's milk and care. As a kitten ages, the probably of successful human intervention increases (If a kitten is days old the chances of success are better than if it is only hours old. If the kitten is a week old, or is old enough that its eyes have opened, then the chances are very good to successfully bottle feed). These kittens were hours old. I knew that I needed to try to get them to bottle feed, yet my primary objective was to get Sara to take over. Somehow I needed to communicate to Sara that her job was not over. Somehow I needed to get her to show an interest in her kittens.

At first I tried paying attention to the kittens and touching them. Sara was unmoved by this. I wanted to show Sara that if she wasn't willing to be a mother to her babies, that I would be the mother. I wanted to draw out a natural competition/jealousy. In order to do this, I sat right in front of Sara, looked her in the eye, and picked up one of the kittens. It fussed at first, cried out a little, and then accepted the bottle. It was not until Sara heard a sucking sound that she reacted. The reaction was instant and was communicated in Sara's eyes. It was as if her spirit was saying: "Hey, that's my baby! That's my job!!" Sara got up and came right over to me. I reassured her and positioned her with her babies. Much to my relief she immediately allowed her kittens to nurse.

From that moment on, Sara was an excellent mother. My belief had fortunately been correct, in that Sara needed to understand that these kittens had survived. Once she realized that they were alive she was more than up to the task of caring for them. Indeed, Sara was very attentive and loving toward her babies. She seemed to take to the first born more than the others, and I wondered if this was because this little one resembled her. As the days turned into weeks, I began to think about the task of finding homes for everyone. It is relatively easy to find homes for kittens, but finding a home for Sara was going to be a bit more challenging. I felt sad for her because she had finally had a healthy litter of kittens, and now I was going to take them away from her. This just didn't seem fair to me. Sara and I would frequently chat about what was to come of her and her kittens. I sat with her one day and made yet another promise to her—that she could keep one of her kittens and that I would find a home that would take her and the kitten. Sara was very clear about which kitten would remain with her, as she had bonded with the one who resembled her. This made sense, as the two black and white male kittens were personality plus and would easily be adopted. Likewise, the gorgeous blue- eyed long-haired light brown (Siamese seal point) female would quickly be claimed. It was this plain tiger-striped female with the anxious personality that would be hard to place. She was named Jane, and she never left her mother's side. Indeed, the two were never apart.

As predicted, the three kittens were placed in homes very quickly. The two males went to the same home, and the gorgeous female went to a home where she was clearly going to be pampered. Even though I did the best to find good homes for them, I worried about whether they would be given the best of care. Sara noticed their absence, yet seemed to adjust relatively well. She seemed grateful to have Jane by her side. I reassured Sara that I would keep my promise. Yet, despite my best efforts I could find no one who would take them both. Occasionally someone would show an interest in Jane, but not Sara. Then on another occasion someone would want Sara, but not Jane. Weeks went by, then months. By the third month I had given in to the idea that Sara and Jane were going nowhere and would become part of my family. I had integrated them into the house without any problems. Sara was a gracious guest. She had lived amongst other cats before and quickly became part of the group. I didn't give it another thought. One day, about six months after she and Jane were integrated into the house, Sara came to me and stared into my eyes. She was very anxious and had an urgent look about her. It occurred to me that she was still waiting on her fate, and that I had neglected to tell her that she was home. I assumed that she knew, yet she was clearly communicating to me significant distress with regard to her housing issues. It was as if she had waited patiently all this time and now needed to know what was going on. I apologized to her had assured her that her and Jane were going to remain with me. There was a calmness that washed over her, as if I had communicated something that she had hoped for and waited to hear.

Sara integrated well into the house. Despite the fact that she had been an outdoor cat, she was pleased with the safety and security of the house and never had a desire to go outside again. Sara and Jane were virtually inseparable for two years. At two years of age, Jane began to rapidly lose weight. Then one day Sara became aggressive toward Jane and I knew something was wrong (animals within a pack will turn on a sick member, which is most likely about preserving the health of the pack: i.e., the weak must die to preserve the strength of the group). I immediately took Jane to the vet. The vet took x-rays and came back into the room with a look of disbelief on her face. At two years of age, Jane's entire body was loaded with cancer. There was nothing that could be done, accept the humane thing—which was euthanasia. The vet believed that Jane may have been born with the cancer, or had certainly developed the cancer shortly after birth. This may have explained why Sara had been so attached to Jane. It may also explain why Jane was such a nervous being and why she had been so attached to Sara. Sara was devastated at her loss. She went into a period of mourning that I have never observed in an animal. For over a month Sara would sleep on my head at night (something she had never done). Other than that, she was almost lifeless. I reached out to her and did my best to console her. It took months, but eventually Sara recovered from her loss. She went back into a period of depression a year to the day that Jane died. Again, she responded well to loving support.

Today, Sara is relatively well-adjusted. I say "relatively" because she has a couple of behavioral issues that speak to a traumatic past. The first is that she absolutely panics if the food in her bowl runs low. I mean, if she can begin to see the bottom of the bowl she launches into an all out panic and comes to me in order to alert me of the crisis. When I refill the bowl she will inevitably binge and then purge—as if she has to eat as much as possible in case there is a shortage of food again. The other obvious neurosis is that Sara pulls her hair out. This is a psychiatric disorder in humans, called trichotillomania, and it appears that Sara has this disorder as well. She regularly pulls on a tuft of hair and spits it out, leaving her coat looking a bit blotchy with semi-bald patches. Other than these two issues, Sara is very happy and content. She has been rather extraordinary in her ability to communicate with me. I know there are skeptics that will insist that I have projected meaning onto Sara, yet I am quite convinced that Sara is able to relate to the world in ways that most humans deny possible. She has taught me that we as humans do not have the slightest clue with regard to the way that animals relate to the world. She has showed me again and again that there is a higher level of functioning that goes beyond basic instincts. This is a sensitive being that is capable of communicating and relating to the world in an intelligent manner. I have been blessed by her presence.

## Chi

He was a little black cat, approximately one year old, and full of 'piss and vinegar'. Because of his propensity to cause trouble, my partner had named him "Baby Bad Boy." At first, I thought she was kidding, as I could not fathom naming any living creature "bad." Much to my amazement, that was his name. My partner advised me that he was bad because he was constantly scurrying about, fighting with his step brothers (also felines) and frequently sneaking out the back door and disappearing for days at a time. Baby Bad Boy was not exactly a planned adoption. As the story goes, my partner's son had been at the home of a friend, where there were a number of kittens running about. Her son had picked up this little black kitten and was petting it, when a team of law enforcement officers started coming down the driveway (apparently with intent to do a drug raid on the parents). Her son shoved the kitten in a coat pocket and bolted out the back door. When she discovered the kitten in her son's room, there was no opportunity to take the kitten back. It was now hers by "proxy."

Integrating cats within a household can be very difficult. My partner had three cats, and I had five. Despite the fact that I had successfully integrated cats throughout a span of twenty years, it became evident that these eight cats were just not going to get along. Baby Bad Boy was relentless in his antics and stalking behavior. It would be one thing if he was attempting to engage in play, but that was not the case. He was rather aggressive and was actually looking to intimidate and obtain dominance. It was beginning to look like a reign of terror—something my cats were not used to. My rule in the house has always been "no fighting." It was a simple rule that generated peace in the home. Baby Bad Boy was having nothing of this rule, and I was becoming tired of the fighting and screaming.

This one particular morning, Baby was on the war path more than usual. By 8:00am he had virtually hunted down and attacked all of the cats, and had even turned on me. I was at my wits end, but had to rush off to work—determined that I would have to come up with a strategy to address the behavior during the day. At the end of a long day, my partner and I returned home to find a horrific scene. Baby Bad Boy was lying unresponsive on the floor in the kitchen. He was in a pool of his own urine. There was no blood, and no mark on him, accept for what appeared to be saliva around his mid-section. The rest of the cats were highly distressed and hiding. Nova (my Doberman) had this look of remorse and guilt—as if to say "I'm sorry, I didn't mean it." Nova had assigned herself as the peace maker and had been getting in the middle of the fights in an attempt to break them up. It appeared that things got out of hand, and that Nova had maybe mauled and shaken Baby Bad Boy.

Baby Bad Boy continued to lie unresponsive on the floor. He was clearly in shock and there was a high probability that there were internal injuries. I gingerly placed him in a crate and my partner and I headed for the vet. On the way, I called my vet to alert them of our pending arrival—only to be advised that another emergency had just arrived and the vet was scrubbing up for surgery. To my dismay, I was referred to another vet in another town. Time was of the essence. My stress level was obviously high, as I had this young cat that was not mine, that was near death, and that my dog had injured. I tried to prepare myself for the worst, as I didn't know if Baby Bad Boy would make it to the vet, let alone survive. I wondered if my partner would ever forgive me, would move out, would file suit. There was a lot to be concerned about—let alone the welfare of this now pitiful Baby Bad Boy.

I did not like the response that we received when we walked into the vet's office. The techs were nonchalant. I had called in advance to advice them of the situation. It appeared as if they were all in slow motion. It was not as if the place was packed. It was after hours and quiet. I don't even recall seeing any other patients in the waiting area. Yet my partner and I waited in the exam room with Baby Bad Boy, who was lying motionless on the stainless steel exam table, for what seemed like an eternity. This cat was lifeless, with a fixed gaze, and was clearly fading fast. We stood in the exam room for twenty minutes without the vet coming in to make an assessment. I really believed that they knew this cat was going to die and decided to allow that to happen. I was about to leave the room and start screaming for them to get in there and look at the cat, when I realized that Baby Bad Boy had stopped breathing and was fading away.

I can't explain what I saw, or felt, other than I knew his spirit was leaving his body and he was in the process of crossing over. He was dying right in front of me. I just wasn't willing to accept this—not like this, not at the hands of my dog, not when he was so young. It just wasn't right. I got down to eye level with him and yelled: "BABY!!" Bam! In an instant it was like the life slammed back into his body and his pupils focused on me. I said: "Don't you dare!" He stayed focused on me for the first time in over an hour. I began to stroke him and sent him love through my eyes. The vet appeared soon after this and whisked Baby away for x-rays. My partner and I talked about the sensation that we had of Baby leaving his body. It wasn't just me, as she had witnessed it as well.

The vet came in with the x-rays, which revealed no broken bones. In fact, she had no diagnosis, other than shock. She put Baby on IV fluids and kept him overnight for "observation." I prayed throughout the night. The next day I was called and told that Baby Bad Boy was "ready to come home." I was in awe. This cat had essentially died on the table and started to "cross-over" and now he was "ready to come home." What came home that day was a totally different cat. The "Bad Boy" in Baby was gone. He was placid, affectionate, and not bothering any of the other cats. Nova initially greeted him, and then stayed far away from him.

The other significant change was that Baby seemed to have imprinted on me. Something happened in that veterinary office. Prior to that moment, Baby really had no attachment to me and rarely gave me the time of day. I was a non-entity in his mind. After I 'called him back' so to speak, Baby attached himself to me. He was now prone to looking lovingly and gently into my eyes. It was clear, even to my partner, that he was now "my cat." This was fine with her, as she had never really liked him. I was not looking for yet another cat, yet this one had clearly declared himself to me. I was always willing to make room for one more. What I was not willing to do was to call him "Bad Boy." I shortened his name to "Baby" for a while, but that seemed a disservice as he got older. The name also didn't do him justice. This cat was full of spirit, full of energy. He was a bit impish, but in a good way now. I decided that a more fitting name was Chi, which means 'energy' in Chinese. Chi was the perfect name to describe this ball of energy. Chi has been a "soul mate" of sorts. He was on his way to the other side and came crashing back into his body on my request (ok, on my demand). He reminded me that we are souls in "skin suits" and that there is so much more than the flesh. He is here "on loan" and I am grateful for his decision to be a companion.

# CHAPTER FOUR

# THE GIFT OF SECURITY

For much of my life I lived with a sense of fear. There was always this sense of vulnerability to predation. It was a constant sense of unease. It was not that I didn't believe that I would not protect myself if attacked, as I have rehearsed many times in my mind fighting off an attacker. It was more about not being able to let down my guard, or my vigilance. There was a time in my life, while living alone, when I returned to my efficiency to find the door slightly ajar. I knew in an instant that I had been burglarized because I would never leave the front door open. I'm not sure what was worse, having cash and sentimental jewelry taken from me, or the knowledge that someone had been in my home. I suddenly felt wide open for attack, with the need to protect myself. I've never owned a gun, simply because for much of my life I was so suicidal that I was more likely to use it on myself than on an intruder. I may not have owned a gun, but I did own an axe! With an axe I wouldn't try to kill myself, but I sure was willing to use it on someone else. The knowledge that someone had been in my home and that they could return at any time was enough for me to literally sleep with an axe (by my side) for well over a month. After that, the axe was sitting by my bedside, ready for use.

About six months after this burglary, I met someone who worked for the Humane Society and she moved in with me. She was fond of Great

Danes (as was I) and was waiting for a Dane to come into the shelter. She came home very excited one day, and asked me to come to the shelter to see the Dane that had just arrived. I was hesitant, as I lived in this tiny little efficiency that had no yard. This did not appear to be the time to adopt a dog. Days passed and Chris continued to plead with me to come see the dog. When I arrived at the Humane Society, Chris was busy in the clinic and I was instructed to walk through the kennels to see the Dane. Apparently, there had been no interest in the dog and the staff could not understand why. I went from kennel to kennel, seeing all sorts of mixed breeds and purebreds.

The Great Dane was in the very last kennel in the back of the building. When I came upon this thing I was in shock. Please understand, I've been around animals all of my life. I've seen Great Danes before. This was a GREAT Dane. The polite way to put it was that he was "large for the breed." The only thing that flew out of my mouth was: "Holy Shit!!" This was, of course, uncensored and rather loud and seemed to echo throughout the kennel. I was relieved that it was a time when few people were looking for pets. I also realized, almost instantly, that this colossal animal was hurt by my reaction. Here was this massive animal that looked more like a horse in a tiny stall than a dog in a large kennel, and he just appeared so embarrassed to be stuck in such a place. He looked so unhappy, so depressed, and so shame-based—like he couldn't understand what he had done wrong to end up there.

My heart went out to him instantly. I looked at the identifying information about him and learned that his name was Buckus and he was five years old. He was a purebred Great Dane with fawn (tan) coloring, weighing 175 pounds. In fact, this massive creature was 6'3" when he put his front paws on my shoulders. Chris came to the kennel, all lit up with excitement and wanting to know "what I thought." My reaction quickly wiped the smile off her face, as I stated: "What do I think? I think it's HUGE." I tried to appeal to her sense of logic. This thing needed a very large fenced in yard. In fact, a farm with a lot of horses seemed a much more appropriate placement than a tiny little efficiency with 6 cats and no yard. She was not convinced, assuring me that we could take him on long walks. We took Buckus outside to the 'acquaintance yard' that was fenced in. This was where Buckus came alive. He was regal, confident, and absolutely majestic. I began to see his glory and started to rationalize how we could make a home for him. I went from 'this is impossible' to 'we'll get a house with a yard.' I turned to Chris and told her we needed to think and talk about this. The smile returned to her face. Buckus, on the other hand returned to his pitiable state when he saw that it was time to return to his kennel. He nearly broke my heart when he looked over his shoulder at me as if all hope had left him. My final words to him that day were: "You're killin' me. I'm not promising you anything, but we'll think about it."

I thought about how we could pull this off. I thought about how nice it would be to go on long walks in a neighborhood that was rampant with crack use. I thought about how nice it would be to move into a house with a big ole fenced in yard. I thought about how nice it would be to give this colossal giant a dignified home. I thought about how it really was possible to pull this off. I also thought about the fact that we needed to find out if he was non-aggressive toward cats. That was now the only thing standing in the way of adopting Buckus. The next morning we performed a "cat test." This is a nervous moment where a few staff members gather around in an enclosed area with the dog to be adopted and a kitten from the Cat Kennel, to observe how the dog responds to the cat. This is done in a professional manner, with proper training, and with the safety of the cat in mind at all times. It's still a tense moment, albeit a necessary one, as it is the only way to see how a dog will react to a cat. Buckus passed with flying colors, as he not only showed no aggression toward the kitten; he seemed rather neutral toward it.

Buckus was neutered (a requirement at the Humane Society) and within 24 hours I was bathing him in preparation for taking him home. Bathing Buckus was a lot like washing a car. The more I got to know this dog, the larger he seemed. This was without a doubt the biggest dog I had ever come across. He got the same reaction from people every time someone saw him: "Wow!" There are just some universal responses that defy much verbiage, and "Wow" seemed to cover it. It got to be comical. Getting Buckus home was also comical, as I had a tiny little Isuzu pickup truck, and Chris had a Volkswagen Fox. Buckus was beaming with happiness when he saw he was going for a ride. Even the indignity of getting crammed into the tiny cab of my truck was not enough to take his joy away. He was going home and he knew it.

The cats absolutely freaked when they saw "the horse" enter their domain. They looked at me like: "Mom are you crazy! What is this thing!" and then they ran for cover. It took days for some of them to come out from the safety of their hiding places. I felt so bad for them and understood their fear. Buckus, however, was such a gentleman. Despite his gargantuan size, he had the ability to lie very still in an unimposing manner. It wasn't long before the cats began to trust him. In fact, as it turned out, Buckus loved the cats and they loved him. It was not uncommon to find the cats curled up by him. I even had a kitten (Rosalita) that would chase his tail, grab it, bite it, and bounce off of Buckus like he was a fun house. Buckus tolerated this like a proud Father. All was well in our tiny little efficiency.

All was well, that is, until we started taking Buckus for those walks. This very docile, placid, mammoth creature turned out to be aggressive towards any human that came within a fifteen foot radius of us. At first I was flattered, as it was like having your own private body guard. I lived in a neighborhood that was drug and crime ridden, so having a body guard was a welcome feeling. The problem was that Buckus couldn't differentiate a potential threat from a harmless person. He would respond with the same force of aggression, regardless of whether it was a six year old child or a thirty year old man. One time, while on one of our walks, a car slowed down and a little old lady in the passenger side rolled down her window to say hello. Buckus lunged at the car with such force that I went sliding with heels dug into the ground. The poor woman looked in horror as the car sped off. Yes, indeed, Buckus was becoming quite a handful. He went from trying to attack people to trying to attack any car that was headed in our direction. It was becoming absolutely petrifying to go for a walk.

We were completely baffled by this behavior, as Buckus had passed vigorous tests while at the Humane Society and had showed no signs of aggression toward humans. He was handled by many staff members, went on many leash walks with volunteers, had people constantly passing by his kennel, passed a cat test, and went through surgery—all with no signs of aggression. In the canine world it is essential to establish leadership. The "Alpha" is the leader of the pack, and it is vital that the human is the Alpha and not the dog. It was clear that Buckus had designated himself as the Alpha, and who could have blamed him. He was clearly the strongest, and was also male. By the laws of nature, he was in charge. We had to get this under control, yet it was rather difficult because Buckus was stronger and seemed oblivious to normal training techniques. Chris tried taking Buckus to training at the Humane Society, but he was too aggressive to be in a group with other people.

We had a real problem on our hands. My biggest concern was the lunging at the cars while on walks. I was attempting behavioral techniques to change his behavior, and not feeling very hopeful. One particular day I was feeling very frustrated and becoming increasingly angry at his attempts to attack oncoming cars and my weakening strength to hold him back. In a moment of helpless rage, at the exact moment a car was passing by and he was lunging, I reached down to grab Buckus by the head. Instead, my elbow came crashing down on his head as I was shouting "No!!" Until now, nothing had been able to get his attention. Until now, that is. Buckus stopped dead in his tracks and came to an abrupt halt, looking at me in bewilderment. Somehow this negative reinforcement had been timed perfectly. One time was all it took. Buckus never again lunged at a car. Finally, I could take him on walks without worrying about him getting killed by a car.

Unfortunately, the same kind of behavioral management techniques were not working for his aggression toward humans. We were able to improve on his behavior slightly, in that Buckus was able to stop lunging at people. However, we couldn't get around the fact that we had an aggressive dog on our hands, and we had to stop people from attempting to pet him. As long as people looked, and didn't get too close, Buckus was fine. Come within ten feet of either one of us and Buckus saw that as a potential attack. Whenever we had friends over, Buckus would have to be locked up in a room or kept on a leash next to us. He was deceiving because he looked so friendly and harmless. One time (after moving to that house with the yard) we had the Director of the Humane Society over for dinner. Buckus was put on the patio upon her arrival. He was looking at her through the sliding glass door, wagging his tail and smiling. She knew Buckus and kept assuring us that he was fine, and to let him in. We gave it a try, and Buckus came in at full charge, pinned her against the corner wall, and had her upper arm in his mouth. While he didn't pierce her skin, he obviously scared the crap out of all of us. This was a woman who had dedicated her entire life to animals. She was an animal expert, could read their behavior, and had no fear. If anyone knew animals, it was her, yet here she was pinned helplessly against the wall with a dog that at one time let her grab him by the jowls and kiss him. Go figure. We went back to trusting our knowledge that this dog was dangerous if allowed to be near other humans. He was like a loaded gun. Treat it with the respect it requires and it won't hurt anyone.

Throughout the years with Buckus it was an act of vigilance to make sure he didn't hurt anyone. Fortunately, while this was concerning, it was also manageable. There was one occasion, though, when Buckus' aggression came in handy. Chris and I were out walking Buckus late one night. It must have been sometime around midnight. There were no street lights on our street (something I usually quite enjoyed) and the moon was out just enough to see silhouettes. We had just rounded a corner and from a distance I saw a pack of young men (their gait gave them away). Gangs were not uncommon in the area, and their body language told me this was a group looking for a victim. Apparently they only saw the silhouettes of two women walking. There were about six of them. Clearly no match, even if we had been men. The group split in half, which also signaled trouble because it meant an attack was imminent. What this gang did not know was that we had a bodyguard. I felt Buckus tense up, watched his ears twitch as the group split, and smiled with the knowledge that he had everything under control. I didn't know whether this group had guns and knives (which they probably did), but I did know that we had the element of surprise on our side. All of this happened in silence, accept for Chris' whisper to me: "Do you see what they're doing?" I quietly acknowledged, and we watched as the group silently began a wide circle within about a twenty foot radius of us. Buckus went ballistic. It took both Chris and me to hold on to him. We instinctively didn't want to let go—both for his protection and ours. The gang was caught off guard and I heard a chorus of: "Holy Shit! They've got a dog. Let's get out of here!" This tough ominous group took off running, not to be seen again. Buckus did not let up until the last one rounded the corner and was out of sight. We were safe, no one was harmed, and Buckus had saved the day. He was my champion and my hero.

As the years passed with my protector I began to realize that the constant fear that I had always known had converted to a continuous feeling of safety and security. It wasn't that I was naïve and believed that no harm could come to me, it was more a sense of relief that all was well with the world. Buckus gave me an incredible gift, a gift of internal safety that stemmed from his constant protection. I was now free to interact with life, to be a part of the world with which I lived. It is a freedom that I did not believe I'd ever have the luxury to experience. I owe that freedom to Buckus.

I had resigned myself to the fact that Buckus would be aggressive all his life. The routine was to warn people to stay away from me and not to try to pet him. I never let my guard down and never tried to introduce him to anyone. We had a party one day and the plan was to keep Buckus in the garage. I had him all set up with a big mattress, food and water, and explained to him what was going on. As guests would arrive we would tell them where Buckus was and not to open the garage door. One of the guests wanted some club soda, which we didn't have, and so I went on a beverage run to the local grocery store. When I came back I was shocked to learn that while I was gone apparently not all the arriving guests learned where Buckus was and to stay away. Two of the guests had decided to give themselves a tour of the house and had ended up in the garage meeting the "sweet dog." My partner found one of the guests not only petting Buckus, but with his head in her hands inches from her face. Neither of these guests knew of his aggression and he was nothing but the gentle and loving Buckus that I had always known. From that day forward, Buckus never showed any signs of aggression. I cannot explain what occurred, other than to say that it seemed like one day he just realized that there was no need for the aggression.

Buckus was by now an old man. This colossal being, this grand specimen, had developed a problem with his spine that started to weaken his hind legs. While able to walk without assistance, Buckus could not climb up stairs or step up into a car. Sometimes his back feet would lock up and his hind legs would be temporarily paralyzed. For the most part he was ok, but he was not the Goliath I once knew. We set out at sunrise one morning for a quiet walk. Upon our return I decided to weed a small flower garden by the patio. Buckus was full of joy and seemingly recounting his days of youth. He was bounding around the yard with the enthusiasm of a puppy. I was getting such a kick out of this. It was adorable to watch him behaving in such a playful manner.

As Buckus tired from his romp around the yard, he began to lie down and roll around on the grass. My back was to him, and I would turn around occasionally and tell him to be careful. You see, there was a canal in our backyard. Canals are common in South Florida, which is where I was living at the time. Some of these canals have steep drops, and are full of a muck that has a silt-like quality to it. The canals were also full of water moccasins (a venomous snake also known as the cotton mouth). My maternal instinct told me to keep an eye on Buckus and to redirect him away from the canal. He was still in his glory, with a huge smile on his face, as he rolled on his back. Twice I told him to be careful. Twice I turned to check on his whereabouts. Then I heard the splash.

Panic washed over me, as I turned to see my mighty dog floundering in the depth of this canal. Buckus had a panic in his eyes that told me he was in trouble. His back legs were so weak that not only could he not get out of the canal—he could not keep his large body afloat. Buckus was going to drown if I did not get him out. Without hesitation I jumped in after him. Having been trained as a lifeguard during my adolescence, I was able to grab a hold of him and get him closer to the shore line. The problem was that Buckus weighed more than I did. The bottom of the canal offered no support to heave Buckus up. In fact, my feet would sink inches into the muck, creating suction when I tried to walk. I had 175 pounds of dead weight. My first attempt to rescue Buckus failed miserably. I looked around to see who might be watching and who I could call on for help. It was 6:30 in the morning, and no one seemed to be awake, let alone outside. I made a second attempt to hoist Buckus up, with the same sinking results.

Poor Buckus was in complete terror. The poor guy was trying desperately to paddle with his front legs. This was of no help to me, as it was the back legs that I needed to help me get him to dry land. I was in trouble because I was now running out of strength. I had tried twice to dead lift 175 pounds out of a mucky canal. I believed that I had one more try left in me, and then I'd have to start screaming in the hopes that someone would hear me. (This did not seem likely, as windows and doors are sealed to almost soundproof in South Florida due to the need to insulate from the heat.) I prayed for strength, and with a determination not to fail somehow I managed to hoist Buckus up onto dry land. To this day I don't know how I accomplished that. I just know that I was not going to let Buckus drown in that canal. Needless to say, we were both exhausted after that ordeal. Other than a bruised ego, Buckus was ok. Poor thing had gone from pure bliss to ultimate panic in a matter of seconds.

Buckus and I had a few more months together. He was aging as gracefully as a large breed can. Their life expectancy is relatively short due to their size (7-9 years) and Buckus was now nine years of age. Our last evening together was a paradox. There was nothing about that evening that was part of the norm. Normally, I would arrive home from work, feed Buckus, and go on a quick walk. This was a two story condo, and as Buckus could no longer climb stairs I would kiss him good night and retire upstairs. On this evening Buckus and I went for a long peaceful walk along the banks of the canal. Upon our return, we sat on the lawn and watched the sunset. This sunset lit up the sky in a magnificent orange. It was a glorious sight, very soothing to the eyes, and full of peace. Buckus was content and enjoying the spectacle as much as I. It was a quality moment that is frozen in time. It was just me and Buckus, enjoying nature and feeling the gratitude of our companionship. I sat there on the lawn with my arm around him, enjoying the final moments of that day.

When it was time to go inside, Buckus did not want to come into the house. This was highly unusual. He wanted to stay on the patio and actually refused to come in. I allowed this, only because he seemed so at peace. I retired for the night, and went upstairs. I had fallen asleep watching the TV and woke up at 10pm. I decided to get up and get a drink from the kitchen—something I never do. I'm the kind of person that does not get up once they get into bed. But this night was different, and I found myself wanting a drink from the kitchen. As I got to the top of the stairs I heard myself think: "What will I do without him?" Two steps later, I was asking myself: "Why am I thinking such a thing?" When I got to the bottom of the stairs I heard Buckus in distress. I ran to the patio to find him coughing and in respiratory distress. He was in acute pain.

I rushed Buckus to the emergency vet, only to learn the distressing news that Buckus had something called Bloat. This is a condition in large breeds (like the Great Dane and even horses) where the stomach twists, cutting off the blood supply. The condition is very painful, and the prognosis is very poor. It can be usually be prevented by raising their food and water bowls (which I had always done) and can also be caused by something as simple as rolling on their back. The vet sedated Buckus and attempted a procedure to correct the condition, with no improvement at all. The only option was surgery, which the vet told me did not offer a good prognosis. Apparently, even if the stomach is 'tacked down' it can still twist up all over again. I would have spent any amount of money if I believed it would have saved Buckus' life, or even extended it. I would have paid off any amount the rest of my life if it could have meant a good outcome. What I had was a situation where Buckus had come to the end of his life expectancy, with a condition that had a poor prognosis and would likely cause continued suffering. I couldn't bear to put Buckus in a position to continue suffering just so I could have the possibility of holding on to him a little bit longer. It seemed selfish to do the surgery, yet I desperately wanted to keep him alive. I agonized over the situation and ultimately came to the decision that I had to do the selfless thing. I couldn't live with myself if I allowed the surgery, only to further his pain and suffering. The decision to euthanize was gut-wrenching, and while I still believe it was in his best interest, I'll never know if the heroics of surgery would have been successful. What I do know is that Buckus' life was coming to a close, and that his passing would have come soon afterward. The paradox for this day was that it was so full of peace and so full of pain. I was allowed a moment of complete and total gratitude and solace, watching the sunset not only on the day, but on my hero's life. I could not have been more fortunate to have that moment in time, for I will never regret those final moments with Buckus. It was a gift from Spirit which allowed me to accept the Order of things, even though what occurred was completely unacceptable to me. Thy will, not mine, be done. Blessed be thy love, thy gifts, and thy presence. Blessed be Buckus, and the many gifts that he bestowed upon me.

# CHAPTER FIVE

# THE GIFT OF ABUNDANT LOVE

There were many feral cats on the street where I lived. A feral animal is a domestic animal living in an untamed state (usually outside). Basically, these animals are wild and fear humans just as a wild animal would. They are typically the result of unwanted housecats (or dogs) that were abandoned to the streets and have reproduced into small colonies that are usually not very healthy. It is a sad statement for irresponsible human behavior. I decided to do something about the overpopulation of feral cats on my street for two reasons. One was that there were so many of them that the situation was going to get exponentially out of control. The second reason was more for my own sanity. If you don't know this, cats are rather amorous creatures. A female cat in heat can mate with many males, and each male can fertilize the female—resulting in many different fathers in one litter of kittens. What takes place is like a mating frenzy, which ends in a lot a caterwauling (screaming) on the female's part. I really didn't care if she was screaming in ecstasy or pain, as the sheer frequency and volume of screams was just too much for me to withstand.

This was not my first introduction to feral cats. While vacationing in the Florida Keys I came across many feral kittens at a Marina. It was late in the evening and I saw about six kittens and started toward them. A boat captain stopped me in my tracks and told me not to bother—that these were feral cats that actually refused food from humans. I thought to myself: "Oh yeah, watch me." I went home that night and returned the next evening with some fish that I had cooked on the grill. I sat down with my open foil pack and patiently waited. Out of the corner of my eyes I could see little noses twitching as they absorbed the aroma of my fish. The smell was too tantalizing to ignore. I barely breathed as the kittens inched toward me.

The first to reach me was offered a piece of the fish. Its nose barely touched the fish, as it recoiled with the reality of fear and jumped back a step or two. I tossed the piece of fish toward the kitten, and it readily gulped the tasty morsel up. I proceeded to toss small pieces toward the rest of the kittens. The fish was so tasty that the kittens began to summon up the courage to get closer. Within minutes they were all eating out of my hands. With a gentle presence I began to stroke one of the kittens on the top of its head. This strange sensation was clearly a first, and welcomed a bit hesitantly by the kitten. I continued to gently pet this little one until the sense of touch became an understood gesture of love. The kitten leaned into this affection, as I now used two hands to caress it. There is a photo of me caressing this feral kitten, with a look of sheer ecstasy on its face. Another photo taken moments later shows me with a huge grin on my face, as I sat amongst the very same kittens who had never allowed anyone to feed them, let alone touch them. It was a moment of glory that I attribute to the universal power of Love and the graciousness of trust. Don't underestimate the power of unconditional love. It is within you, deep within your soul. It has the capacity to heal and transform your life, and the lives of others.

Now I was faced with the task of managing my own neighborhood feral colony. The first step in the taming process was to feed the cats. Initially the cats would not come to feed when I was present, but in a short period of time I was able to sit quietly within a five foot radius while they ate. There were probably close to a dozen cats—all of breeding age. There were long hair cats, black cats, orange cats, and black and white cats. The biggest cat was a large black male, with a big ole head, that I called King. He was clearly the Alpha cat of the colony, and would be the first to eat. Once he had his fill and left the bowl, the others would come around and feed.

After a while I set up 'Have a Heart' traps that would contain the cats without injuring them. I'd put a sedative in their canned food (given to me by my vet) and once captured I'd whisk them off to the vet to be neutered. Once the cat was neutered, I'd release it back into the neighborhood. I figured this way the cat would not be able to reproduce and both of my problems would be solved. The young adults I would take back home and tame, and then find homes for them. This way they had a much better life than 'living on the streets.' This whole project took a lot of time and money, but was worth the effort. Some would argue that all of the cats should have been euthanized. I understand this logic, as it may be the kindest thing to do. However, at the time, I believed that these cats were managing well on their own (as they had been long before I had arrived on the scene). I figured if they could live out their lives without continually reproducing, then that would be the most humane thing to do.

One of the female cats was very smart and was able to avoid the traps that I set. She was clearly pregnant, and I waited for her to have her litter so I could round up the kittens and adopt them out. When I hadn't seen her in days, I decided to go looking for her. The neighbor's back yard was more like an untamed field than a yard. There was no lawn to speak of—just overgrown bushes and fruit trees. In the very back corner of this yard, under an overgrown fruit tree, I spotted a little black kitten. I was excited at my find, thinking I had found the litter. I crept upon this little one while it was sleeping, and was shocked to find that it was all alone. This was odd, as there should have been four or five more. Feeling eyes upon me, I scanned the yard and saw the mother cat at the other end of the yard. It looked in my eyes, blinked, and then hurried to another yard (probably to the rest of her kittens). I had the strangest feeling that this cat had just thanked me, as if I had lifted a burden off her. There was no terror in her eyes, just a calming presence of relief.

I turned back to the kitten that was peacefully sleeping, and as I placed my hands on it this little tiny fur ball looked at me in total horror and began writhing with fear. I grabbed it by the back of its neck, as its mother would, and held it to my stomach as I ran back to the awaiting cage. This poor little thing was crying and hissing and was just beside himself in fear. It took about an hour for him to settle down before I could hold him and reassure him that I meant no harm. He was so tiny he could fit in the palm of my hand. He was jet black, with a white cross on his chest. The cross was just two lines, one that stretched from one armpit to the other, and the other line a perfect perpendicular that dissected the horizontal line. It looked as if God had painted a cross with just two strokes of a brush. This kitten was old enough to have its eyes open, which was a good sign because it meant it was over a week old and had a good chance of surviving through bottle feeding. He couldn't have been much older than a week, as he still had jet blue eyes—the color that all kittens are born with. I knew instantly who his father was, as this tiny little thing had a huge head. This was King's son.

About three days before this I had witnessed a horrific event. I was driving along Route 441 right before rush hour and witnessed someone literally open their car door and throw a young cat onto the road. Traffic was going at about 45 mph. I pulled over and frantically jumped from my truck in an effort to stop traffic and rescue the cat. My gut sank as I watched the young gray cat get run over. The traffic was responding to my frantic waves and slowed to a stop as I went to the kitten. It was about six months old. I took it to the median and held it in my arms and prayed over it as it crossed over. I told him I was sorry for the cruelty of humanity and blessed his life. I wept for this little one whose life was obviously not cherished as he so deserved. Out of dignity I gave him a name, Joshua, and then walked back to my truck with him. I was in shock by what I witnessed, and had been on my way to my therapy appointment. My poor therapist had to deal with me when I got there. I was still clutching this cat, all bloodied, and with no emotion. I explained that I knew he was dead, but wanted her to confirm that for me. She did so, and we put him in a bag to rest in peace while I had my session. I took Joshua home with me and buried him with the respect and dignity that he deserved. I prayed for his peace, and prayed for an opportunity to save a life instead of bury one.

Now it was three days later, and I had this little black kitten with the white cross. Without any thought, I named him Joshua. I now realize the religious symbolism in all of this, but at the time I was rather clueless. The next time I saw my therapist I brought Joshua. She asked me if I knew what Joshua stood for. I did not. She said that it was another name for Jesus. When I showed her the white cross blazed across his heart she went pale.

As it turned out, my Joshua was a very sick kitten. I took him to my vet the day after I found him. Joshua had an eye infection, an upper respiratory infection, mange, and four types of worms (tapeworms, roundworms, hookworms, and coccidia). The vet tried to let me down gently, telling me 'not to get my hopes up' and essentially telling me that it was unlikely that Joshua would live more than a few days. She gave me medication to treat everything. If he lived, the two major problems would be the mange and coccidia. Apparently, Joshua was so young that the dosage required to treat him would kill him. So, he required a very low dose that would take months to cure the mange and coccidia. Joshua had a fighting spirit and, after all, his father was the Alpha King. I just believed that this little one was going to make it.

Coccidia is a nasty little intestinal parasite that causes a rather foul smelling diarrhea. Needless to say, caring for Josh was a daily practice in unconditional love. Because Josh was still supposed to be nursing, I had to bottle feed him every two hours. This meant that Josh had to come with me to work every day. I set up a little nursery in an empty storage room and would tend to Josh between clients. After each feeding, kittens need to be stimulated so that they will urinate and/or defecate. While this can be messy, it was at least something that was controlled and planned. As Josh got older and started to void and eliminate on his own, I would be met at the nursery with an awful stench. Once cleaned and fed, Joshua's purring was a constant reminder to me of the value of his life and the privilege to assist in bringing him to health. I got very good at timing—timing his feedings, timing his bowel movements, timing his medications.

Joshua was so small that he could fit in the sleeve of my shirt. He would nest in the sleeve of my upper arm, finding warmth and comfort, and sleeping in between feedings. I started to sing an old song, originally sung by Billie Holiday. I became familiar with "My Man" as a little girl when I would listen to the Barbara Streisand album from the musical "Funny Girl." Now, this song was not a perfect pick, as it speaks to an abusive relationship. However, the verse spoke to my love for Joshua. The lyric went like this: "Oh, my man, I love him so. He'll never know. All my life is just despair, but I don't care. When he takes me in his arms, the world is bright all right." I sang this to Josh throughout his nineteen years of life. It was 'our song' and was dedicated for the profound feeling of love that I had for him and that he returned to me.

As time went on the true color of his eyes were revealed to be a brilliant bronze-gold. Josh grew stronger every day, and as the days turned into weeks his health also improved. By the time he was six months, all of his health problems were resolved. I continued to bring Josh to work with me and he quickly became a welcomed sight to the clients. Joshua was a natural therapy cat. He would greet my clients and then curl up with a pillow and sleep throughout the session. He went through a stage during his adolescence when he was very rough. He wanted to run and play and was a ball of energy. I had a 78 year old woman who was coming to see me for the first time and I was afraid I would have to crate Josh; for fear that he could easily scratch her delicate skin. To my amazement, Josh seemed to know how delicate she was, and he was as gentle as possible with her. She was delighted with him and responded with a glowing smile.

There was another client that I was working with for a couple of years that had never been able to show any kind of emotion. We had been sitting on the floor during sessions in order to create a more relaxed environment. This was a young woman who had a significant history of loss and abuse during childhood. During this particular session, Josh was sleeping under a pile of pillows in the corner of the room. The client was now in crisis, and the pain of an abusive past was coming to the surface. She was initially very loud as she tried to verbalize her pain, and then she began to release her pain through tears. It was an excruciating moment of suffering that opened a door to healing. As we sat in silence I reached over and placed my hand on top of hers. Joshua began to stir from his pile of pillows and crawled out from the corner and walked over to us. He lay down by this client and then placed his paw on top of ours! The client was in awe of this, as it was an act of compassion—something that she needed and absorbed into her healing process. Joshua remained still, purring all the while, while this client released her pain in a timeless moment of validation and support.

Joshua was very helpful to me as a therapist, and I quickly learned to watch his reaction to people as they came in the door. He would alert me as to their current emotional state. Those that were angry he would greet and then go off to a corner and go to sleep. Those that were depressed or in crisis, he would lay by their feet throughout the session. I was facilitating a women's group, and found Joshua's skills highly accurate and fast. As the group would begin I would watch Joshua to see where he would 'settle in.' He would invariably lay down next to the woman in the most distress. This was not always obvious, as sometimes people where a façade of calm when in reality they are hurting. Week after week Joshua would lie down next to the woman that I needed to focus on. He was really that good, and quickly became my co-therapist in the group. One evening, the women all filed in with what seemed like a whirlwind of energy. I felt chaos and crisis. I hadn't paid attention to Joshua, as there hadn't been time. One woman after the other shared her crisis and distress. I wondered if it was a full moon. I had a limited amount of time and knew I needed to somehow address them all. I wondered which one of these women was in the most distress, as they all seemed equally needy to me. I looked to see where Joshua had situated himself. To my complete amazement, he was smack dab in the middle of the circle! This was a perfect metaphor for what was going on, as there were so many crises that they were literally 'centered' in the room. Each client was like a spoke on a wheel that was spinning from an axle. Josh nailed it alright, as they were all equally distressed. I seized the moment and called their attention to Joshua. We shifted from individual distress to the dynamic of the group energy. At that moment these woman began a shift from the problem of individual pain to the solution of group validation and support. This really high stress, energy sucking evening became a pinnacle moment in a shift toward universality. Joshua was not just a therapy cat, he was becoming a teacher and I was a highly receptive student.

Josh had a soothing quality to him that was contagious. He was a greeter, a healer, and a very social being. His presence could not be ignored by anyone. Josh came with me to work for over 1 ½ years. My career took some twists and turns, requiring that Josh remain at home. This was a difficult adjustment for him, as he truly enjoyed working. However, he was just as needed at home, and quickly became the Alpha cat in the house. He was as huge as his father. He also had an appetite that wouldn't stop. Monitoring Josh's food intake became a daily task once he was retired from his work as a therapy cat. It was not possible to leave food out, as Joshua would eat it all, leaving nothing for any of my other cats. He would become aggressive when hungry, and was prone to attack the others in order to draw attention to the fact that it was feeding time. All human food had to be sealed and placed in cabinets. On one occasion, I came home to find that Joshua had jumped onto the kitchen cabinet, knocked a loaf of bread to the floor, and had then dragged the entire loaf of bread down the hallway to my bedroom, where I found him in my closet eating the bread. I had a closet "foodaholic" on my hands! Josh would have been morbidly obese if I had not controlled his intake. As it was, he was very large and well over 20 pounds. He was massive. It was typically the first response when someone met him: "Oh my God, he's huge!"

Joshua's inherent ability to demonstrate compassion never ceased to amaze me. There was a time when I volunteered to foster kittens for the Humane Society. Sometimes kittens would come in too young to be adopted out and would require two-four weeks of fostering. On one occasion a young Siamese mother and her six kittens were brought in to the shelter. The kittens were too young to adopt out and it was decided to place mom and kittens in a foster home. I was delighted to have this guest in our home and even more pleased that my six cats were gracious hosts. Josh, in particular, seemed to take to Mom and her babies and would lie down near them. Unfortunately, the mother cat became very ill with a fever and died within 24 hours of being brought to my home. I was in shock as this was completely unexpected. Now I had six kittens that needed to be bottle fed and tended to. To my sheer amazement, Josh took over as a surrogate mom. This male Alpha cat, allowed these kittens to nurse on him. Now, obviously they were not getting any milk, but they were comforted by this and quickly took to Josh as their mother. Josh would clean them and discipline them and watch over them much like a mother cat would. He did most of the work with regard to fostering these kittens. I could tell he was exhausted by them, yet proud at the same time. The kittens remained healthy and within about six weeks they were all at the Humane Society and quickly adopted out.

Josh remained my hero throughout his life. He was a constant source of comfort and companionship. He was a special soul that touched my life—he was my rock. He aged, for the most part, with grace. It was difficult to watch this aging process, because it signified the impending passing of a great presence in my life. While I had time to prepare, I could not get myself in a place where I could be ok with losing him. It's funny because Josh left my life as he came into my life—incontinent and requiring constant clean up. It was a final reminder that he was worth every inconvenience. What I'm left with are special memories of a spirit that was beyond description and truly a blessing in my life. Joshua was a small creature with a large spirit that acted as a healer, leader, and teacher. He will remain forever in my heart and soul.

*Part 3:*

# GIFTS FROM SPIRIT

# CHAPTER 1

# FROM SPIRITUAL BANKRUPTCY
# TO SPIRITUAL AWAKENING

<u>Disclosure</u>: *The text within contains information pertaining to the progressive nature of my alcoholism and my journey into recovery. Part of the journey involved my participation a 12 Step Program. In no way do I represent this Self-Help Program, nor shall I ever intend to. The sanctity of a 12 Step Program requires that members maintain anonymity at the level of press, radio, and films. This section is my story, my interpretation, and my perception. I am not presenting this account of my alcoholism as a member of any particular 12 Step Program. I am presenting an account of my alcoholism as a personal story, which includes giving credit to a twelve step program that saved my life.*

## *Everything is Under Control*

My first semester at college gave me the opportunity to drink without any kind of supervision. I initially started drinking on Friday and Saturday nights. This seemed perfectly logical as the week was officially over and it was time to play. Sunday was the day to 'buckle down' and get ready for classes. Then my friends convinced me to come out on Thursday nights. At first this seemed wrong, but I quickly realized that as long as I was 'caught up' with classes it was ok. After all, I was just getting a 'head start' on the weekend. Then I would be called to come out drinking on Wednesday nights. Since everything was under control, it seemed reasonable to go out with my friends. Then I was going out to bars on Tuesday nights, and this seemed perfectly normal because 'everyone else was doing it.' By the time I was going out to bars from Tuesday-Saturday it seemed rather irrational not go out on Sunday and Monday nights. I mean, really, isn't it silly not go out on those two nights when you are going out every other night? It's not like I was an alcoholic or anything. I was just partying with my friends. No problem.

Somewhere along the line, and rather quickly, alcohol started becoming a necessity. I needed it to get my mind off my problems, to relax, to socialize. I seemed to function better with a slight buzz. I turned my closet into a liquor cabinet, and began drinking every day. I had a speech class at eight in the morning and I was terrified to speak in public, let alone in front of a class. A couple of strong Black Russians a few minutes before I headed to class worked quite nicely. I was mellow and relaxed as class would begin. It was all part of the "better living through chemistry" philosophy on life.

When my second roommate requested a room change, I was surprised. I thought we had been getting along just fine. She said it had nothing to do with me, yet would not offer any other explanation. I took it personally; then pacified myself by stating I was glad to be rid of her. Now maybe I could finally have the place to myself. I took over the entire dorm room, lined up my empty bottles and cans along the window sill, and began living like a pig. Laundry was a drag, so I just didn't bother to do it. The higher the dirty pile became, the more proud I was of my accomplishment. When I ran out of clean clothes, I just picked something to wear from the dirty mountain of clothes on the floor. I washed my bed sheets two times that year (once each semester).

One evening I was blasting my music, with a six-pack just about finished, when I heard a knock at the door. When I opened it there was a small woman standing there, smiling politely. She introduced herself, said that she had been informed my room was available, and was interested in meeting me. I was quite dumb-founded as I invited her in. The RA (Resident Assistant) had not informed me that anyone would be stopping by. My room was like a bombshell. There were a half dozen pizza boxes full of moldy crust, along with the empty bottles and the dirty laundry mountain. She did not seem a bit distracted by the condition of the room. She said that she was miserable with her roommate, and desperately wanted to move out. When it was clear that she had full intentions of moving into my pig pen, I could not help but think that she <u>must</u> be desperate.

When Ginny moved in she continued to be full of smiles, despite my lack of warmth toward her. She was highly intelligent, very friendly, studied long into the night, and had a very positive outlook on life. She would have made an exceptional friend. She was a beautiful, kind person. She deserved to be with someone who was kind in return. I was too busy being a drunken fool to give her the time of day. It annoyed me that she seemed to be concerned about me, and that was the last thing I needed. I was doing fine on my own. I was sorry she had ever knocked on my door.

Ginny was an inconvenience. She was 'in my space' and there was no hiding how I was living. It may have been the norm for college kids to drink, but I knew full well that my drinking was not exactly the norm. I went to the bars every night and drank throughout the day. I used the money from my athletic scholarship for booze, and when that was all gone I began calling home for money. I would say I had found a sweater that I "just had to have," and would manipulate my mother into sending more money.

Alcohol no longer got me high. It helped me to function. It helped me to feel normal. There was no more euphoria associated with drinking—no matter how much I drank. I felt depressed all the time. I had several different counselors at the mental health center, and nobody seemed able to help. I wasn't exactly honest about my drinking, but I maintained that it was their fault because they never asked. They also never noticed my hands. As depressed as I was, I was also very angry. I sought relief through punching things. Many of the gyms at the field house had padded walls, and I would go down there and use them as punching bags when no one was round. It made me feel better. I was miserable, and this was a great outlet for my pain.

I started needing to punch things more often, and began using my bunk bed when Ginny was at the library. The top mattress was at eye level, which was the perfect height. One night I was really getting into it, and deriving quite a bit of pleasure from my workout. I was interrupted by a knock at the door. The RA came to see what the noise was all about, as the student in the adjacent room had complained to her about the constant banging on the wall. I told the RA that everything was fine, and felt nervous when I saw her eyes widen. She walked into the room and looked in horror at the blood-stained mattress before her eyes. I had not even known I was bleeding. There was no way to talk myself out of this, as she had caught me literally red handed.

I was called in to see the Dorm Director, who advised me that she was fully aware of my drinking and "self-mutilating behavior." Apparently several students had voiced their concerns throughout the semester. The Dorm Director was going to mandate me to counseling, and seemed relieved when I informed her that I was already attending. She was still concerned about my drinking. We worked out an arrangement with my RA. I was to clean out my closet of alcohol and store it in my RA's room. If I "needed" a drink, I was to go to her and talk to her about what was bothering me. If I still wanted a drink after talking to her, I would be allowed to have one. I was all for it, and thanked them for their help. I cleaned out my closet and handed over the booze, and the next day I bought a new stash and hid it. I complied with their policy, as well as my own policy (which was to drink as I had been before their "intervention.") I stopped hitting the mattress, and instead I focused my "workouts" down at the gym. I taped my hands so I would not bleed as much when I "boxed." I learned and memorized Ginny's schedule, as well as the RA's, and planned my drinking around them. Everyone seemed much happier. I didn't worry them so much, and they were finally off my back.

One evening, while I was out drinking on my own, I got drunk and felt suicidal. I went searching for one of my friends to talk to at one of the high-rise dorms. When I got to her room I realized that it was foolish to be looking for her there, as it was Friday night and she would be out partying. I was out of hope and walked over to the window in the lounge area. The window was open and as I sat on the ledge, looking more than six stories down, I took a long look at myself to determine if I had the courage to kill myself. I had decided to jump from the ledge when I noticed people pointing at me from the ground. I heard someone coming down the dorm hall, so I climbed back inside and headed to my dorm. I was definitely considering suicide, but not in front of an audience.

As I staggered to my room I was completely shocked when I found two coaches from my high school sitting there talking to Ginny. I was obviously drunk, had just come off the ledge of the high-rise dorm, and they had arrived completely unannounced. I was even more disturbed when they informed me that I had written to them, as well as some of the high school students, stating that I was an alcoholic. I had absolutely no recollection of that. In fact, it seemed totally out of character. I was not an alcoholic. I drank a lot, but I did not have a problem. It was under control. Yet there they were. They had driven over four hours, from Long Island, to check on me and to see if they could help. I agreed to talk on the condition that they buy me a six-pack. We sat drinking for a while, and then went to sleep.

It was decided the next morning over breakfast that I should definitely cut back on my drinking. My concerned friends were trying to tell me that it was possible to go out and have just one drink, and have a good time. I was all for it, and suggested we go to my favorite bar that evening to try it out. We went and, as planned, I had one drink. I sat there feeling smug, and also feeling no effect from the alcohol. My tolerance was too high to be effected by one drink. I assured my friends that it was, indeed, possible to have just one drink. They agreed that I seemed fine, so it seemed equally fine that I have just one more. I knew that one of the two enjoyed drinking, and that all I needed was to get her going, and we would be partying all night long.

When I opened my eyes it was daylight. I did not know where I was at first. The last thing I remembered we were all sitting around the bar that we went to for one drink. I realized then, that I was on my bed. It frightened me that I did not know how I had got there. My friends were asleep on the floor, and Ginny had already gone off to the library. I felt sick. I had a humdinger of a hangover. I was a bit surprised to learn that we had done our share of bar-hopping the night before. I was informed that I had danced on a dare with a rather unattractive male, that I had busted down the door to the DJ because she was not playing the songs I wanted to hear, that I was so intoxicated that I could not walk and they had to carry me a half mile to the dorm, and that when they finally did get me to my dorm floor, I spent quite some time sitting on the floor in the bathroom stall. I was vomiting and intermittently thrashing my head against the wall so violently that one of my coaches sat with me on the floor so that she could stop me from bashing my head open. I had made quite a scene, all right. I had embarrassed myself, and proved to my coaches that I was way beyond any help that they could provide. They left that day, even more concerned than when they had arrived. I was more concerned about my hangover.

My first semester eventually came to a close, and not a day too soon. I was out of money, had even sold my textbooks so I could buy liquor, and was ready for a break from the intensity of the semester. The semester was intense not because of studying or exams, in fact it had become quite routine for me to skip class. The semester was intense because my drinking had become a full time job. My friends couldn't seem to keep up with me anymore. They would stop drinking and get ready to go home for the night before I had my fill. I was out of money, and so desperate for more booze that I would steal tips from the bar. If there were no tips I would get down on hands and knees in the stale beer puddles on the floor, and look for change that had fallen during the evening. Sometimes the bar was so crowded it was almost impossible to move. I often wondered if some of the puddles contained urine as well as beer. It certainly smelled that way, and was highly probable as the lines to the rest rooms were intolerable if one had to go that badly. In fact, the "Dark Horse" was so jam packed with people every night that you wouldn't know if someone was 'urinating in public." Yet, even that thought did not deter me from searching through the muck on the floor. The most important thing was to find enough coins to buy another drink.

My drinking progressed throughout the next semester. Getting home from the bars was becoming a difficult task. On one occasion I woke up in the early morning hours to find that I had passed out in a snow bank. I was cold and wet, and somehow had the presence of mind to travel back to my dorm. I passed out again under some trees near the building. When daylight arrived I picked myself up and headed into the dorm. Ginny had been worried sick about me. I was incensed when she told me she had filed a missing person's report. I thought she had some nerve. I was perfectly capable of taking care of myself. I managed to hurt her feelings and push her away enough that she finally got the message. She moved out shortly after that incident. I wish she could know me now. I wish I could tell her how sorry I am for being who I was. I wish I could tell her that even though I never let on, I knew there was something very special about her.

## Just One More Beer

Classes definitely interfered with my drinking. I rarely studied, unless it was the night before a test—if I even remembered there was a test. Any attempt at studying was met with absolute frustration, as it was getting harder and harder to concentrate. I could not comprehend what I was reading, and what I did comprehend I usually did not retain. Attending class became somewhat of a hit or miss thing. Mostly, I did not care whether I made it to class or not. In my child psychology class, the professor handed back my mid-term exam and told me she could not understand how I managed to pass.

There was one class that I not only attended, but enjoyed. It was a required course (Health 110) that all students at the college had to take. There were some 500 students taking the class each semester. Most of the professors in the Health Department taught at least one section of the course. I enjoyed the course because I was actually learning something. When we got to the section on alcoholism and drug addiction, I was not exactly open-minded. In the first place, I felt that nobody could tell me anything I didn't already know. My father was an alcoholic—I knew all about alcoholism from watching him while I was growing up.

I decided to attend not because I wanted to learn, but because I wanted to see if the teacher knew what she was talking about. I sat in the back section of the auditorium, and made sarcastic and critical comments to myself. Yet there was something about the woman in the front of the room that made me stop and think. She was the only professor that had managed to get the attention of every single student. It was customary for students to walk out of class before it was over. When Marley taught the class students sat in their chairs until the last minute. She was the only professor that students would openly praise while scrambling to get ready for their next class. She really seemed to genuinely care about the students. Her heart was really into it, and she was intelligent. She always had a line of students wanting to talk with her afterwards. I thought those students were nerds.

I was a bit disturbed by her lecture—something about how alcoholism was not only multi-generational, but how there was strong support for a genetic link. At the end of class I waited in line with the nerds so I could hopefully clarify what appeared to be a gross error on her part. "Excuse me," I said, "Just because someone's father is alcoholic that doesn't necessarily mean that his children will become one, right?" She did not answer me right away, but moved about the stage, gathering her materials from the lecture. Irritated, I repeated the question: "Just because my father is an alcoholic that doesn't mean I'm one, right?" She looked me straight in the eye for a brief moment and then said: "No, not necessarily."

That was not the answer that I had been looking for. Who the hell did that bitch think she was, anyway? Why couldn't she just answer me straight? What was this 'not necessarily' bullshit? She was supposed to say: 'Yes, that's right; you won't necessarily become an alcoholic.' The woman obviously didn't know what she was talking about. I left the auditorium cursing up a storm under my breath, yet a part of me felt a connection to her…as if a voice were saying that when I was ready, she would be there. I thought I was crazy to think such a thing…I went home and got drunk.

By now I was drinking throughout my waking hours. Everything revolved around alcohol. I drank anything I could get my hands on, and loved the taste of all of it. I had started out with a very high-end taste, you know, nothing but the best. The sheer volume and amount of money to support my drinking made it necessary to lower my values, so to speak. I went from expensive beers, to what the college students referred to as "Genny Cream." This was Genesee Cream Ale and it was the cheapest beer that you could buy. My eating habits were very poor, as I preferred to live almost exclusively on pizza, Doritos, and beer. As my drinking progressed, my one or two meals a day was one slice of white bread, with a thin spread of mayonnaise. I would vomit as soon as I started feeling nauseas from drinking. I believed that it was a foolproof way to avoid a hangover the next day. It also helped because I would feel relief immediately. Once I had vomited, I could resume drinking within minutes. It worked like a charm.

There were days when a case of beer wouldn't get me a good buzz, and other days when two or three beers would get me drunk. I thought this was great because I was drunk and it didn't cost as much money. The problem was my drinking was costing my health. Reverse tolerance (needing less and less alcohol to get the desired effect) is a sign of liver damage. I was also having blackouts (alcohol-induced amnesia) frequently. Sometimes I would be "missing" hours, sometimes, days. Upon awakening the first question was "Where am I?" The second question would be: "What day is this?" The third question would be: "What happened?" After a while I stopped trying to find out the answers to those questions. It just didn't matter. Never mind the fact that I came out of a blackout one evening to find myself hugging the porcelain wheel on the bathroom floor in the stall of the men's room. No big deal. Besides, the men's restrooms were always cleaner than the women's restrooms. It was getting to the point where I couldn't live with alcohol and I couldn't live without it. On three occasions throughout the year different people tried to intervene and three times I turned my back on their offer of help. I was so progressed in my alcoholism that I was now spiritually bankrupt. Despite this, I was not finished drinking

No big deal that I was becoming increasingly paranoid, that I was losing friends, that I was bloated and looked 6 months pregnant. Gone were the days of drinking to feel high. Gone were the days of drinking to feel normal. When I picked up a drink, the objective was to feel less depressed…and that was it. When I would wake up in the morning I would find one of two things: I was either still drunk from the night before (something I thought was the best thing since ice cream because it meant I had a head start on the day), or I had the shakes. My whole body would be trembling, and my hands would be shaking like a leaf. Nothing a Black Russian could not resolve. Everything was still under control, all right, only it was alcohol that was controlling me.

My freshman year came to a close, and two days after my cast was removed (an athletic injury that required knee reconstruction) I was heading back home. I dreaded the thought of going back to my parent's house, yet there were no alternatives. I was still on crutches, needed extensive physical therapy, and was in no condition to be securing summer employment. During the day I had the house to myself, as both parents worked. I would mix up anything I wanted from the liquor cabinet, and there was also the keg of beer in the garage. There was always so much booze in the house that it would be hard to notice if anything were missing. I had also established myself as a "college drinker." I was extremely offended when my father turned to me at dinner one night, saying I had 'become just like my old man.'

I went to physical therapy regularly, and was fortunate enough to frequently get a ride from my high school coaches. I thought it was funny when I started getting comments about the smell of booze in the car. When a ride was not available, I never thought twice about drinking and driving. After all, I was in control so I could handle it. I was so in control that I would run red lights, drive recklessly, and be on the receiving end of angry drivers shaking their fists and blowing their horns. I thought nothing of having a 'few shots' (nine, actually, of my kind of shot—none of this one ounce stuff) of Dewar's White Label, and then driving the forty-five minutes it took to get to physical therapy. I would sit in the cold whirlpool watching this black horizontal line that kept moving upward in a continuous motion (the kind of line you used to see on TV sets that required adjusting). I would giggle as I would try to swat it away, knowing all the while that nobody else had this image in front of their eyes.

At night there were parties to attend. Seeing my high school friends again held the promise of good times. I was appalled when one of the guys asked me if I was pregnant. Couldn't he see that it was just a beer belly? What a jerk! My friends did not approve of my drinking. It seemed like I couldn't get through a party without someone saying they were 'concerned' or that I should 'get help.' It was starting to sink in, yet I continued drinking.

I went to one of the last parties of the summer, and became severely depressed. My friend sat me down and told me flat out that I had a drinking problem, and that she wanted me to get help. She was very insistent, and wanted me to go for help before I went back to school. I told her about the professor from my Health 110 class, and promised that I would go see her when I got back to school. I was ready to get help, ready to realize that there was a 'problem' with my drinking.

About two weeks before I was to return to school, my mother approached me, stating that she was 'concerned' about my depression. She had made arrangements to institutionalize me in a psychiatric hospital (Bellevue). I knew that if I ended up there, my life would never be the same again. I had to remain calm. I had to be convincing. Something took over, and I informed my mother that I had already been to see our physician, had been placed on medication (a tranquilizer), and would be getting counseling at school. She was pleased to hear that I was getting help for myself. She stated that if things did not get better, she would continue with plans to hospitalize me.

I was two months shy of my nineteenth birthday, had been drinking alcoholically for two and a half years, had appeared to have reached 'my bottom,' had the threat of hospitalization hanging over me, and was seriously considering the advantages of suicide. I went back to Cortland in search of this professor named "Marley," hoping that she would be the one to point me in the right direction.

When I reached Marley's office, it was packed with students. They were all standing around joking and having a good time. I wanted to turn and run, and never come back. At the same time, I had this 'now or never' feeling that pushed me toward her desk. She looked up at me and smiled. I took a deep breath and said: "I was wondering if I could set up an appointment sometime this week." She began flipping through her calendar and stated: "Sure. Am I your advisor? ("No.") Are you one of my students? ("No.") Are you a Health Major? ("No."). She looked rather perplexed, but seemed to know better than to ask any more questions in front of all those students. She gave me an appointment, and as I walked out the door I felt a flood of relief.

I was trembling the next time I stepped into her office. She cleared some books off a chair that was next to her desk, and asked me to sit down. As I sat in the chair I felt more like an observer, as I listened to myself speak. I began by praising Marley for her lectures in the Health 110 class. I also shared with her that I was impressed with her teaching skills, and the way she connected with the 110 students. I told her she seemed worthy of trust. Having said all of that, I left my observer's position and began to give a truthful account of my drinking history. I even told her of the tranquilizers my physician had prescribed, and my plan to attempt suicide. She listened intently and without judgment, and then came up with an intervention plan. She called and set up an appointment for me with an alcoholism counselor who worked for the County, she contracted with me to get rid of the tranquilizers as soon as I got back to my apartment, and she set up two more appointments with her so I would have continued contact while I waited for my appointment with the counselor. I felt safe with her. She never once told me not to drink, or to 'just have one.' She was smart. I never would have gone back if she had.

The day finally came for my first appointment with the alcoholism counselor. Andy had long hair that was tied in a pony-tail. He was very tall and thin, and chain-smoked. The fact that he looked like a hippie-leftover from the sixties made me feel at ease. He sat down with pen and paper, and told me he wanted me to tell him what brought me to his office. He took notes while I told him about my life. It took two sessions, and I was as honest as I could be. When I was all finished, he put his pen down and asked me if I wanted to know what he thought. He took me over to a chart on the wall and proceeded to point out many of the things I had told him. When he got to the bottom of the curve of this chart, he showed me what was waiting for me. Death was right around the corner, and he believed that I was very close to committing suicide.

I felt relieved that someone finally understood the seriousness of the situation. He told me that I needed to be hospitalized in a detox facility. I told him I thought he was nuts—I was not addicted to alcohol. I just had a drinking problem. He told me that I had until a certain date to think about it. Then he set up another appointment with me, and sent me on my way. He informed me that my chances of making it were not good.

In my poetry class that week, I came across a poem in my textbook that struck a familiar chord. Following is an excerpt from that poem:

> Ale, man, ale's the stuff to drink
> For fellows whom it hurts to think:
> Look into the pewter pot
> To see the world as the world's not
> And faith, 'tis pleasant till' tis past
> The mischief is that 'twill not last.'
> Oh I have been to Ludlow fair
> And left my necktie God knows where
> And carried half-way home, or near,
> Pints and quarts of Ludlow beer:

Then the world seemed none so bad,

And I myself a sterling lad;

And down in lovely muck I've lain,

Happy till I wake again.

Then I saw the morning sky:

Heigho, the tale was all a lie;

The world, it was the old world yet,

I was I, my things were wet,

And nothing now remained to do

But begin the game anew.

A.E. Houseman, <u>Terence, This is Stupid Stuff</u>.

## Journal Entry: September 10, 1981

*Things have certainly changed the past three weeks or so. Do I have things out of perspective? Do I know what I'm doing? Who can I trust? Do I dare talk to anyone? If I do will I be sorry I did?*

*I am so confused, yet I clearly know what I must do. I just want to get it over with. I am not weak. Yet, I am not strong either. I want to go to my friends and ask them their opinion. Yet, I don't want a soul to know what goes on inside me. This time I want to keep to myself and not cry out for help. Instead, I'll get help through professional people. But, I don't want that either. I want to stand on my own two feet. I don't want the humiliation of this problem.*

*Being depressed is one thing, but when you add the drinking problem it becomes another thing. The humiliation enters at this point. After talking with Andy, it seemed that my drinking was a major factor in my life—a focal point. I felt as though he almost had blown the whole thing way out of proportion. For all I know he tells everyone he sees what he told me.*

*I'm OK. I really am OK. I don't need any help. I just need to fade out, to get away. The past few days I've been wondering what it would be like to quit school and go south, or west, and find a job. It's possible. I've considered not coming back next year. Why bother? I don't know what I'm doing yet, and I'm wasting money staying here. But when I think like that I just ask "Why bother living at all?"*

*Nobody has ever come out and told me that I **need** to do something. Nobody has ever said that I need help, shouldn't do it myself, and they'll help me. Nobody has ever taken me aside and said: "Look, this is what's happening to you, this is* *why, now here's something to do to help yourself." Nobody, that is, except Andy. In a sense, he's giving me an answer. I don't know that I want an answer. I don't want help. But, I do. Please leave me alone and let it go away and fade out. I'd rather shrivel up and die than say "There's something wrong with me, I have a problem, I am weak." I'm strong and I can beat out anyone. Yet, this is not true. Be honest with myself? Am I? How will I know if I am? Trust someone else? I'm afraid to. I'm confused. I'm alone, yet there are so many people willing to help me.*

## Journal Entry: September 12, 1981

*"Happiness is a warm gun."—The Beatles. John, if you're talkin' 'bout suicide…how true. Now we've got Bob Seager. He's cool too. Yes, I'm buzzed. I love it. What a good buzz.*

*Yet, and this is the point, I'm still depressed. Vickie, listen to yourself. You're at a level of happiness. You're happy. You'd like to stay like this all the time. Yet, even at this level, when you're happy, you're really not happy. You're depressed. You're so elated, yet you want to kill yourself. I want to do myself in. The **HELL** with life.*

*I'm going to detox on Wednesday. I've decided. I'm psyched. There's no hope for me. I'm finished. Why bother. But, I've got to. Maybe it will help. I'm by myself, and I love it. But, I don't. I'm alone. I'm scared. I'm insecure. I admit it. Help me please. Help. I'm dead inside.*

I drank throughout the weekend, and into Monday. I checked in with Marley, and then on Tuesday, September 15, I went back to see Andy. He wanted to send me to detox. I came up with excuse after excuse about why I could not go. He finally made a deal, and I promised to abide by it. If I were to remain alcohol free for one week, and go to as many Self-Help meetings as I could, I would not have to go to detox. If I could not follow through, I would go immediately to detox from our next appointment. I thought it would be a piece of cake. I was shocked when I went through withdrawal. I had the shakes so bad that I would have to sit on my hands during classes so that I wouldn't make a spectacle of myself. I was hearing voices—someone kept calling my name. I was as sick as a dog. It turned out to be one of the most meaningful and spiritual weeks of my life.

## Journal Entry: September 19, 1981

*My first 12 Step Meeting was in Dryden. (Rather ironic, to catch a 12 Step Meeting at 'dry den') Everyone was really nice. Last night they discussed the first of the twelve steps. Each member spoke once. They'd explain when they first admitted that their life had become powerless and unmanageable. I sat and listened for an hour and a half. Each person evoked a different emotion in me. You're not supposed to compare yourself, but some would talk about their jail experiences. I have not been in jail. I'm not that bad off. Some spoke and hearing them made me laugh because I could really relate. But then others spoke and while I didn't outwardly cry, I sobbed on the inside. Something inside said: "Yes, yes, you are an alcoholic."*

*Maryann spoke of her blackouts and it really hit home. How many times in the last year did I not only wake up and not remember what I did the night before, but not even remember how I got in my own bed? That scares me. Look at me now. My hands are shaking. I'm going through withdrawal. How many times have I come home and absolutely died because someone close to me saw me drunk? How many times have I come so very close to killing myself?*

*Hearing what they said wasn't funny. It was the sad truth. How can I not admit I'm an alcoholic when it so clearly controls my life? I sit back and half of me does admit it. But the other half can't bear the thought of never drinking again. I'm so young. I'm only eighteen. It's really not that serious. SHIT MAN! WHY CAN EVERYONE ELSE DRINK WITHOUT A PROBLEM BUT I CAN'T. That gets me so pissed. No. No, No, No, No, No. **NO!! I AM NOT AN ALCOHOLIC. NOT ME.** I can handle it. Who cares, anyway? I was depressed way before I started drinking and I'll be depressed even if I stop. So why stop? I've gone four days without an ounce of alcohol. Me an alcoholic? No way, man.*

*At the end of the meeting the chairperson gave me a white poker chip because it was my first meeting. She told me to carry it with me wherever I go and if I'm ever in a bar or with drink in hand, maybe if I take the chip out and hold it, I won't drink. The chip is significant in that it's a symbol of all those who struggle every day NOT to drink. It's a symbol of all those people whom I heard speak last night. People who don't drink anymore, but who struggle not to. Am I really an alcoholic? Maybe. I haven't decided yet. No wait...I haven't admitted it yet.*

## Journal Entry: September 21, 1981

*I still cannot concentrate. I read words and pages in my textbooks and none of it sinks in. I'm trying desperately to concentrate, but I'm finding this so extremely difficult to do. I didn't do much as far as studying this weekend. I did do one thing though—I **didn't** drink.*

*I went to another 12 Step Meeting on Saturday. I walked downtown to the Grace Episcopal Church. There were a lot more people there this time. I didn't feel as comfortable as I did at the first meeting. I wanted to leave as soon as I walked in. I couldn't handle another night filled with alcoholic stories. One guy sitting next to me hadn't had a drink in 21 years. The guy on my other side hadn't in five years.*

*I sat and listened to these people for another one and a half hours. Again, I had such mixed emotions as anger, sorrow, relief, denial, self-pity. I looked around the room at all those people. They were all your average, everyday, American citizens. Suddenly it occurred to me the vast number of alcoholics there are. It's not so degrading. These people are all very nice. They're self confident and have all experienced the same thing. Through sharing their experience they achieve sobriety. All you have to do to belong is have the desire to stop drinking. That's not so hard.*

*Well, the meeting ended and I just wanted to get the hell out of there. It was all too real for me. The guy I was sitting next to gave me a couple of pamphlets to read. His name was Terry and he seemed really concerned and went out of his way to be nice. Before I left a woman named Jan came up to me and spoke with me. She gave me her telephone number and address. "Call me at three or four in the morning if you need to," she said. All these people were so kind. They could understand how I was feeling because they, too, had been through it. They were reaching out to me as someone had once done for them.*

*I started walking home and as soon as I got up the street I started crying. "**No. Not me!**" was all I could exclaim. "I can't be an alcoholic. I need to drink. I can't go 21 years without a drop of alcohol. I'm not like my father. Those people in there are all different than me. They are alcoholics. I'm different. I'll drink differently now. I just want to get blasted once a week. I'll just drink one beer. One Lite. They say it's a progressive disease. Well, I'll prove to them and myself I'm not an alcoholic. I don't have any disease. It's not progressing with me. **I'm too young to be an alcoholic.** I have too many good times ahead of* me. *I can't have a good time unless I drink.* **No, No, No, No, No. NO!!! I'm not an alcoholic!"**

I continued to walk home and when I got to campus I sat down on the pavement for a minute. I opened one of the pamphlets, and it read: "Hi, I'm Davy and I'm fifteen, and I'm an alcoholic." I shouted "*Fuck You Davy!!*" I read on…"*I used to think I was too young to be an alcoholic.*" I retorted: "But I AM too young!" I was angry with the pamphlet. My attempt to disprove my own alcoholism through literature proved unsuccessful. I got up, still crying, and continued my walk through campus. As I walked past the dorms, the music blared and students were gathered together drinking beer and laughing. They were having a good time. I became enraged, and then paranoid: "STOP LAUGHING!! It's not funny. Why can you drink and I can't?! It's not fair. Don't anyone come near me. Leave me alone. I'm warning you. Don't come near me. I can't. I can't do it. I can't go the rest of my life without drinking." I remembered some scenes from last semester when we'd all go out drinking. Everyone would end up with beer in hand, arms around each other in a huge circle, swaying back and forth to the music. "That is happiness. I can't take that away from me. I need those good times. I need that beer."

I stopped at the edge of campus. "Where should I go? There's no one to talk to! Everyone went home for the weekend. I can't go to my apartment. My roommates will see I've been crying. "I wanted to go and talk to some friends, and took a step or two toward their house, and then stopped. "They can't tell me if I'm an alcoholic or not. Only I can tell myself that. No one can answer for me."

I started home again at a somewhat slower pace. The tears continued to flow in streams down my cheeks. I was feeling defeated, yet I still wanted a drink. "Just **one** drink. **I just want one beer.** I've gone four days without a beer. That's good enough. I need my beer. **God, please, just one more beer.** I promise if you'll let me have one more beer, I won't drink anymore. But shit, if I drink I'll have to tell Andy. I can't lie. I don't want to go to detox. But please, please, **God—please—**I want a beer."

I was all alone in the parking lot of the Field House, which was usually full of both people and cars on a Saturday night. I stopped and opened the second pamphlet. It asked such questions as: '*Do you have blackouts from drinking? Do you shake when you stop drinking? Does drinking affect school or work? Do you need a drink to have a good time?*' I screamed into the night: "SHUT UP!

*SHUT UP! You're lying. You're trying to brainwash me into believing I've got this disease. You're making the questions up in a way that I'll answer yes. You're lying! I'm not one of you!! You've formed a cult. You're a cult, and you're trying to get me. I'm not crazy. I'm not going to be a part of it. You can't get me!!"*

*I continued to escalate: "Fuck You, God!! Fuck You! Who the hell do you think you are? You're a fucking asshole, that's who. Where have you been all of my life? Why did you put me here? If you're such a loving and All Mighty God, why don't you help me? Why don't you let me die? I dare you!! You're no good. You don't listen to me. You probably don't even exist. Fuck You. I hate you. One more beer, that's all I ask. Just one more beer!! Is that so much to ask for? I promise not to drink anymore. I promise, God. Please? I try to listen to you but you never talk to me. Well, Fuck You!! I don't need you anyway."*

*The parking lot was very large, and as I was midway through I saw something that made me stop dead in my tracks. There in the open, in this empty, cold, dark parking lot was an unopened bottle of Miller Lite beer. It was standing there all alone, directly under a light post. When I got to it I reached down and picked it up. It was cold, unopened, and there was only one. I had received what I asked for. I stood there, bottle in hand, and thought for a moment. I could open it and drink it, and no one would know. No one but I and God (as by now I was pretty convinced that this Being was definitely in my presence). It could be my last beer. I had been given a choice.*

*I put the bottle of beer down and walked away, still sobbing. It was then that I admitted that I was an alcoholic. I was painfully aware that if I were to drink that beer, there would always be just one more. In the end, it was up to me. It was my choice. To live, or to die? I chose life. I've come to realize that for me at least, admitting that I'm an alcoholic is the easy part. Accepting the fact that I am alcoholic is a very gradual process. I know I am an alcoholic, and with each day I will work to accept this fact more and more.*

## The Promise of Recovery

My life changed drastically once I stopped drinking and found support in a 12 Step Program. Suddenly there was direction in my life. This Self-Help Program provided a step by step suggestion of recovery. All I had to do was follow the directions and my life would change. I was told that 'the program' was simple, yet I was warned that it was not easy.

The advice and genuine care that I received from members of this Program was crucial in providing me with the ability to transform my life. I desperately needed direction. All aspects of my life had become unmanageable. I learned that recovering from alcoholism was more than abstaining from alcohol. Recovering from alcoholism meant that I would need to heal physically, mentally (and emotionally), and spiritually. It was a tall order. I believed that if I worked hard enough and did not give up, I too could be released from the daily obsession to drink.

Probably the greatest obstacle to overcome was my resistance toward a spiritual understanding of life. I had been raised Catholic, and while some of the indoctrination from that institution stayed with me (however unwanted it was), I had fought throughout my childhood to refuse to assimilate the glaring (and not so obvious undercurrents) of hypocrisy, discrimination, and prejudice of the "One and Only Holy Catholic and Apostolic Church." I did all the things that I was supposed to do as a Catholic. I had been baptized, went to confession, received communion, went through conformation, attended religious instruction, went to church on Sundays, prayed with my mother when she would light a candle, learned to recite all the prayers we were supposed to learn, etc.

I believed that there was a God, and called it Him because that was what I was told to do. I believed that there was a man named Jesus, and that he was a teacher, suffered greatly, was crucified, and that he had some connection with God. That he was the "Son of God," and was "seated at the right hand of the Father," was something that reeked of a male-dominated culture to me. I took the good that I could find, as some of the teachings had sound values. The rest I left for the believers, the Catholics.

I did not believe in any organized religion. At the same time I did believe there was some Being that was greater and more powerful than me. My 12 Step Program gave me permission to develop my own understanding of a "Higher Power." With that freedom in hand, I set out to discover my own spiritual beliefs. I had more questions than answers, and was very skeptical. I prayed to be open to the answers, should they be revealed to me. My journey was slow and steady. Eventually, the answers would come.

## Journal Entry: October 19, 1981

*I saw Ordinary People for the second time. Wrong! Bad answer. That movie was too much me. I could really relate to the boy in the film. When asked why he wouldn't let himself feel things he said: "When I let myself feel things it hurts too much." I can't count the number of times in the past that I've said that. One other thing hit home that he said when talking about depression: "First I was really down and things were kind of grey. Then it was like being in a hole and the hole got bigger and bigger until I could no longer get out. Then I became the hole..." I've used this very same analogy to describe depression. The tears just streamed down my face while he said that. My eye twitched constantly throughout the movie.*

*When I left, the first thing I told myself was to stay away from a bar. I was at a very vulnerable point. I wanted to drink. I wanted to die. I remembered what everyone says in my 12 Step Program—pick up the phone before that first drink. I called my mentor. I couldn't understand why I went to that movie knowing it was going to cause great pain. She said something that made so much sense: "Sometimes we go back to our past to see the things we didn't and couldn't have. We go to find a happier ending, too." How true that is. It all made sense when she said that. I felt better then.*

## Untitled Poem: October 26, 1981

*I walk home at night with nothing to give*
*But an empty glass, a dime, and a tear.*
*What kind of life is this I live?*
*A life of solitude, depression, and fear.*

*I've been drowning in beer and whiskey,*
*The insanity of it is getting to me.*
*Feeling selfish and full of self-pity,*
*Is so very hard to see.*

*How harsh these words may seem*
*But I've come to realize they're true,*
*Drinking alcohol must forever be a dream,*
*Or, like many, I'll end up dead too.*

*For just today I will not drink,*
*I'll try not to get lonely or bored.*
*But I have yet to find the missing link,*
*Which has been proven to be you, my Lord.*

*The rain falls from the heavens to the ground,*
*God, are these tears you are crying?*
*This alcoholism takes me round and round*
*Please help me grow tired of sighing.*

*I want to hear you, I truly do.*
*But something holds me back.*
*Maybe I'm afraid to place trust in you.*
*Maybe it's faith that I lack.*

*Lord, I need you so much*
*And I want to let you take the lead.*
*Alcohol is a deadly crutch,*
*That leaves a wound from which to bleed.*

*Of this I am thinking as I sit,*
*I know I have got to try.*
*Often I feel I may not make it*
*I mustn't give in, or I'll die.*

*Lord, please be with me today*
*And help me to carry on.*
*Only you can end this dismay*
*And steer me from Misery's talon.*

I also received a great deal of support from my roommates. I was out of the dorms, and living in an apartment with three other women. Terry and I had been on the field hockey team together. She did not understand my alcoholism, or recovery from it, but was supportive of my efforts to get my life back together. She did not drink. Ellen did not drink, either. She would listen to me hours on end as I fought to find a spiritual meaning of life. She also had a very odd sense of humor that I found refreshing. Judy was one of the more optimistic and seemingly naturally happy people that I had ever met. Life was like a party to her, yet she also had the ability to be serious when such was called for. I looked up to Ellen and Judy. It amazed me that they could wake up happy, smiling, and joking.

They teased me unmercifully (and in a good natured way) until I started taking them more seriously and life less so. Their constant commentary on my lack of organization, primitive habits, poor eating habits, and unkempt appearance eventually got through. The standard joke was that it was easy to find me when they got home from class—all that was needed was to follow the trail of clothes. I would disrobe piece by piece as I walked about the apartment, ending up with underwear and a bed-sheet that was wrapped about me toga style.

They refused to be intimidated by my foul moods. I started to change. I started to let them into my life. I even accepted a precious gift from Judy- the gift of laughter. The three of us would sit around the kitchen table and laugh until we cried. My bladder was weak from all the drinking and it took years before I had enough control to laugh without peeing in my pants. We would laugh about that, too. It was OK for me to be human. I did not have to be ashamed that I frequently did not make it to the bathroom. On one occasion I was bolting out of the kitchen in a vain attempt to make it to the bathroom, only to lose control of my bladder in the hallway. I lay down on the floor, and just started laughing uncontrollably, yelling out "I didn't make it!" Judy ran to her bedroom and came out with a rain suit that she draped on top of me, while Ellen held an umbrella over me. It was one of the most compassionate, humorous, healing moments that I have ever had.

I continued to struggle with my new-found sobriety and quest for spirituality. At the same time I was trying to recover academically. It was nearly an impossible task. I considered a leave of absence, but was afraid I would never return. The pressure that I felt was immense.

## Journal Entry: November 22, 1981

*I've slipped mentally. I mean I'm thinking like a drunk. I haven't taken a drink, but you'd never know it. I'm so full of anger. I can't even believe that once* *again I am in denial. I've been trying to convince myself all day that **I am** an alcoholic. I just feel that I'm different. Things were going great and I was feeling so good. I didn't even <u>want</u> a drink. But lately, I've been obsessed with it. Why can't I, anyway? Why do I have this fucking disease?! I can't go through with this Self-Help Program shit.*

*I don't know how to ask for help. It seems so easy for them. I often feel like I'm the only one struggling inside. They really seem like people who have their shit together. They couldn't have been as bad off as I am now. No one can change that much. It all looks like bullshit to me. It's either bullshit or a miracle because it would take a miracle to get a drunk to become a person full of life, God and wisdom. Miracles don't happen. How can I ever be like they are?*

*I know I've only been going to meetings for two months. I know it takes time. But, I'm hurting and in pain and I need something to make me numb. Alcohol used to do that but it hasn't for two months now. I don't have anything to take the pain away anymore. I can't do it myself. That's where God comes in, right? He will take the place of booze. Yet, my mind stays closed to Him. I'm fighting that step and I'm winning the fight because as long as the will isn't there I win. But, in actuality, I lose. I lose because without a spiritual program of recovery there is nothing to take the place of alcohol. Without a Higher Power I still think like a drunk. I'm depressed. I'm mad. I want to drink and feel crazy. I don't want to feel better anymore. Every time I feel better I end up crashing with a harsh thud. I keep trying to exist on a high. It's either feel high or feel low. I haven't been able to find a neutral. I thought I found it these past two months, but I'm beginning to feel that it was all just bullshit. Have I been bullshitting myself, or am I bullshitting myself now?*

*The main thing that consistently ran throughout my head today was that I haven't experienced alcoholism enough yet. I haven't been to the hospital due to drinking; I haven't been arrested. I mean, really, I wasn't in that much pain. I don't need help. But all bullshit aside, I have experienced alcoholism and I know it! It hurts. The emotions that stir within me are so very real. The anger is real, as well as the guilt, self-hate, self-pity, depression, insecurity, fear, etc. Yes, I've experienced alcoholism. Must I now go out and drink and fulfill the "yets" and add to my list of experiences? What for?*

*I need to ask for help. I need to humble myself a little. I need to call my mentor, be honest, and don't be afraid to "say too much." I've got such a long way*

*to go. Will I ever find my way out of this alcoholic maze? Not by myself, I won't.*
*But I might if I ask for help.*

At the end of my first semester as a sophomore I decided to change my major to Health Education. My GPA was at an all time low (2.28), but I was determined to turn things around. My goal was to finish my senior year with a 3.0 average (which would require all A's for the next two years). I improved with each semester, and became confident in my ability to study, comprehend, think critically, question, retain, and express myself. I was very active in my classes. I wanted to soak up as much as the professor was willing to give me. I loved thinking. It was not long before my peers were looking up to me. They would come to me to clarify questions about the material, or for help in studying for an exam. They valued my opinion. I earned the respect of my professors as well.

I also spoke at the college, as well as area high schools, regarding my alcoholism and my process of recovery. It was an excellent experience for me. I learned to feel comfortable in front of a group of people, and to communicate in a manner which would make my audience connect with me. I enjoyed giving of myself to others. Speaking helped me to put things in perspective, while providing a message that I was told was powerful.

At the end of my senior year my GPA was 3.06. While I was happy that I had achieved my goal, I was sad at the lost opportunity to have really excelled academically. I had the ability to consistently achieve semester GPA's averaging 3.6. If only I had my act together those first two years. If only—yet what a miracle that I had come this far. I had to stay an extra semester for my student teaching, due to the change in my major. I refused to attend graduation because I believed if I didn't finish my Bachelor's degree within four years I didn't deserve to attend the ceremony. How unfortunate that I had to punish myself like that.

Judy, Ellen, and I lived together through our senior year. Judy eventually moved to Virginia and obtained a job at James Madison University. Here's a 'God thing' for you. You see, James Madison had been my first choice of colleges to attend. I had tried out for a field hockey scholarship and couldn't wait for the opportunity to play for the team. I had thought it was a sure thing, and needed the scholarship to attend. I never heard from the coach and was crushed that I didn't get the scholarship or the chance to play for her team. OK, so fast forward some six years later. It is an incredibly small world. Judy was now the swim coach at James Madison University and had become friends with the field hockey coach. Judy mentioned my name, and the coach actually remembered me. The field hockey coach said that she never understood what happened. She had wanted me on the team, had offered me a scholarship, and I had turned down the offer!! All those years I thought I had been rejected, and it turns out that I rejected them. I must have been in a blackout. I guess it all worked out as it was supposed to.

Marley had become one of the most important figures in my life. She had been so many things to me: mentor, teacher, and friend. She was by far the most talented, skillful, intelligent, professional, caring teacher that I had experienced at the college, and in my life. She was unfailing in her support and unconditional regard for me. Saying goodbye ripped me apart inside. I gave her the most important symbol of my life: my first year bronze medallion (a customary gift in 12 Step Programs to mark yearly achievements of sobriety), which marked one year of abstinence. I had carried it in my pocket every day for over two years. It was symbolic of all that I had accomplished and become. It also represented a miracle that never would have been possible, had I not walked into her office that September day. Marley had been there with me every step of the way. To this day I consider her to be a cherished gift.

The road to recovery had begun. Drinking was never the answer, just a respite from despair that had made me more hopeless with each passing day. It would be a difficult journey, as the odds of an eighteen year old maintaining abstinence (in a college drinking town) were not good. Andy and Marley later confided in me that at the time they did not believe I would make it. What they did not know was that there was a powerful Influence in my life…an Influence that has been extremely patient and unconditionally loving with me.

# CHAPTER TWO

# ON BEING PSYCHIC

## Dreams

*If I categorized my dreams, I would break them down into those that I never recall, neutral dreams, disturbing dreams, dreams that provide lessons, pleasant dreams, informative dreams, and 'the dream that isn't really a dream at all.' Those would be my categories—listed in order from the most common occurrence to the infrequent.*

### Informative Dreams

In my psychic dreams I usually tap into the lives of those around me. I'll be present with them for a few moments, discussing an event they have recently had, or have yet to experience. It's like I'm right there with them, and I hear and see what is meant for me to learn, and then the communication line terminates. Usually the information I learn is of another's pain, but sometimes it is just information...like what they are thinking, decisions they are making, what's occurring in their lives, etc. When I am asleep, it is as though I become an open switchboard. I would say that most of the information I receive comes as a form of preparation—either to comfort me, or to give me what I need to be able to comfort others. It's like the physical form exists but I'm dealing in a spiritual realm. To quote Pierre Teilhard de Chardin: "We are not human beings having a spiritual experience. We are spiritual beings having a human experience."

I had been working for the county as a substance abuse counselor on the outpatient unit for many years. There was a group of us (approximately 10-12 counselors) that had been working together for many years. Over time we had managed to learn how to appreciate one another, and functioned much like a family. Our supervisor announced during a staff meeting one day that a new outpatient unit was going to be opening up west of town, and that half the staff was going to be reassigned to the new unit. The news was met with groans and complaints, and not surprisingly, no one wanted to volunteer to transfer to a new unit. Our supervisor then advised us that a "top secret" list would be devised and that on a designated date each counselor would be called in to the office and advised of his/her fate.

There was much angst amid the staff regarding the transfers, and many of us attempted to guess who would be the chosen team to start the new unit. Two weeks went by and we were advised of the date that we would all be informed of the final decision. Approximately two days before the meeting, I had a dream. The dream was brief, and was as if I had been brought into the future. I was in my supervisor's office and heard him explaining to me that I was chosen to be part of the new unit. He was apologetic when telling me the news. I recall that the background of the dream was light and in color. There was a positive sensation, and I knew that this transfer was going to be a positive event in my life.

When I was called into my supervisor's office two days later, the events from my dream began to unfold. My supervisor began talking to me in a very formal manner about how the final decision was made. Then he gently 'broke the news' to me in a very apologetic manner. I smiled and advised him that I already knew about the decision and that I was sure it would be a positive outcome. A stern look came over my supervisor's face, as he asked how the information was leaked and who it was that told me. When I told him that I had a dream about it he was at first puzzled, then skeptical. I assured him there had been no leak and that I would keep the information to myself until his process of disclosure was complete.

The experience at Outpatient West turned out to be the best placement that I had while working for the county. It was like being in private practice.

I was filled with gratitude every day that I was there. My supervisor, it turned out, had been chosen as part of the transfer at the old unit. Now, about two years later, he called our staff together and announced that a new unit would be opening in the South of the county and that one or two of our staff would be chosen to transfer to the new unit. The same procedure was to be used, with regard to secrecy. Again, a few days before the announcement, I had a dream. Yet again, in this dream I found myself in a future moment, being advised that I had been chosen to transfer to the new unit. This time, the backdrop was very dark and shadowed. I knew that this would be a toxic environment for me.

When I was called in to the office by my supervisor I sat in a chair by his desk and started speaking before he could. I said: "It's ok. I know. I had another dream. I know that I have been chosen for the transfer. I also know that this is not going to be a good experience for me. I'm not complaining or asking you to change anything. I just need you to know that I'm not happy about this, but I will accept it. I just want to know why I keep getting chosen to go." His answer was simple: "Because you are one of our strongest female counselors." He tried to reassure me about my premonition—that he was confident that I would 'love it there.' I told him I was open to the positive and prepared if that was not the outcome.

My experience at outpatient south turned out to be very dark, both personally and professionally. I think I was there less than a year when I made the decision to resign from the agency after 5 ½ years of employment there. My dream provided comfort to me, as I believed that somehow this was all part of a Higher Order of things. I accepted the outcome, even though I was unhappy about the toxicity of my environment. I learned that I didn't have to tolerate toxicity, and that I could choose to leave even though it meant walking through the dreaded fear of change.

Another example occurred some time ago, while working for an agency that treated the dually diagnosed. I was asleep and had a lucid experience, as if my dream had been interrupted by a visit from someone I had never met. An African American woman, in her late twenties, approached me. She was small in stature and frame, and had a light complexion. She informed me that she was scheduled to begin the program that I was working in. Her admission date was the next morning, and she was not going to attend. She told me that she was not ready to come in. I asked her why, communicating a desire to assist her. She told me that she was frightened, that she couldn't overcome her fear, and that she was going to continue to get high (on crack cocaine). I recall sending love, and telling her that we would be there if and when she became ready. The whole 'dream' only seemed to last seconds— the amount of time it would take to have a conversation.

The next morning, during a treatment team meeting, my supervisor announced that there was an admission scheduled for the day. Before she could provide any details, I blurted: "She's not coming." My supervisor assured me that she had spoken to her the day before, and had confirmed her start date with her. Without censoring what I was about to say, I announced: "I am aware of that, but I know that she is not coming today. She spoke with me in a dream last night." By now, the staff was looking at me in a rather confused and skeptical manner. I provided a description of her height, age, weight, skin tone, and drug of choice. My supervisor was in awe, remarking: "How did you know that? Did you see her? Was she here earlier this morning?" I assured my supervisor that I had never met the woman. The final comment from my supervisor was that she was sure the client would be arriving shortly. The client never arrived, and to my knowledge did not request services again.

## Disturbing Dreams

Sometimes I am informed of a pending death. With regard to celebrities, I was advised of Elvis Presley, Lucille Ball, and Fred Astaire's deaths days before they actually occurred. It was like I saw the newspaper headlines before they occurred. When news of their deaths spread it was of no surprise to me—just confirmation. While I felt sad at the passing of such stellar artists, these losses were relatively neutral occurrences in my life.

During a summer semester break, while staying at my roommate's house, I had a very disturbing dream. Actually it was a nightmare that I knew was a terrifying reality. The "dream" had me literally sit up in bed in a full sweat. I observed a satanic murder that had just taken place. The details were hideous. I knew a young man was dead, and that an animal had been sacrificed. I knew that it involved a group of young men and that this murder was going to make headlines. I knew too much, yet not enough to go to the police. I can't recall anymore if it was the next day or the day after, but the murder made the front page of all of the New York papers. All of the information revealed was consistent with my dream. The information that I had not been given was that the leader of this satanic cult was the son of one of my High School teachers. This teacher was also the head football coach. He was a well known and respected man. He was also a good teacher. I grieved for my former teacher, as well as those who were tortured and murdered in the practice of evil. It was an event that remained in the news for some time. I was confused and horrified that I would be on the receiving end of such an event. I don't even watch scary movies because I cannot stomach violence. To witness a murder seemed cruel to me. This gift that I had felt more like a curse.

Many years later I had a dream about a little girl named Julie M. who was abducted and killed, and dumped in a field. Most deaths I am unaffected by, other than my own brief sense of loss, followed by happiness for the individual's release. With Julie it was a whole other experience…an excruciatingly painful one for me as I was completely helpless to save her, and lacked enough information to pin-point her whereabouts so that her anguished family could finally grieve and give little Julie a dignified burial. I dreamt about her on two occasions. During the first dream I saw the lifeless body of Julie in a field. I could see what she was wearing, and the immediate area she was in. There was tall saw grass and small bushes. The sight was frightening to me, as it had an energy that was filled with evil. When I learned of Julie's disappearance, I was horrified because I knew she was no longer alive. I grieved for the family, as they were appealing for their daughter's safe return. I wanted to contact the police to inform them of my dream, but was afraid I would either be looked at as a suspect or a lunatic. During the next dream I saw a protest outside the police station. There were posters that spoke to the frustration regarding the lack of information and closure. Some were accusing the police of not doing enough to find little Julie. I saw Julie's immediate family among the protestors. Days later, while watching the news, I watched a replay of my dream. The hair stood on the back of my neck, and I felt a tingling sensation throughout my body, as the event appeared exactly as it had in my dream. I felt sick inside, because I hadn't communicated what I knew in my heart to be true. Weeks passed before Julie's body was discovered by a couple of hunters in a field on the outskirts of the Everglades. The description matched my dream—down to the clothing she was wearing. After that experience I asked that my gift be removed from me. I didn't want to know about murders or experience another person's pain if I was not able to help in some capacity. To have some detailed information, but not enough to be of any help, was almost torturous to me. Since then my psychic dreams have been scarce. It hasn't been until recently that I've asked for that channel to reopen—with the condition that I can be of service to others with the information that I receive.

## *Dreams that aren't really dreams*

I had been working with a young adult woman (age 18) whose mother had terminal cancer. Her mother was well known in the community and had been ill for a long time. She worried about how Claire (fictitious name) was going to function without her. Claire was very depressed and anxious and also had a history of addiction. She was attending 12 step meetings, yet her sobriety was very shaky due to her mother's condition and pending death. There was a maternal instinct in me that felt very protective of Claire. I felt like my spirit was hovering over her. This must be a literal translation, because I had a series of dreams that indicated I was 'hovering' so to speak.

During sleep my spirit left my body. I know this only because I heard myself thinking: "Cool, I am out of my body." I appeared in a parking lot, near a lamp post. I suddenly realized that I was hovering over my client and another female that she was with. The two were alone and had a serious conversation. It was late at night, and no one else was around. I could hear the conversation and knew how my client was feeling. They both got in the car, which was a convertible, put the top down, and drove north on I95. I could hear the songs that were playing on the radio. I followed them quite a while above the car, gliding through the air. This was all effortless and without conscious thought. I was just an observer, hovering overhead, with a feeling of total neutrality. I had never had this kind of experience before. It really wasn't a dream, but more like an out of body experience. It was like flying. It was such a freedom to be out of my body and moving freely through space and time. I have since learned that this is known as Astral Travel.

When I awoke the next morning I recalled everything as though I had been in a wakeful state. Since I had never experienced this before, I wondered if it had really occurred. During my next session with Claire I decided to try to validate the information I had. I explained to her that I had a dream and that I wanted to see if the dream was accurate. I explained in detail what I had observed. The car that I saw was the friend's car—a car I had never seen. It was a convertible and they did stand exactly where I saw them. Claire got very uncomfortable when I told her the nature of their conversation and even more uncomfortable when I told her they were on I95, which direction they were traveling in, and which songs played on the radio. In fact, I could see that poor Claire now had way too much information to process, as she stated in fear: "Where were you when all of this was going on? You had to be there!!" I reassured Claire to the best of my ability and explained that I have had paranormal experiences throughout my life.

My astral travel did not stop with that one experience. I had two more occasions, both involving Claire. When Claire's mother died I traveled to their home. I had never been to their home in person, did not have their address, and didn't know where they lived. However, I appeared in their home and could tell you the layout of the home and the way that daylight came through the windows. I checked on Claire on both occasions, finding her grief-stricken yet functioning. Claire validated the layout of the home, looking at me in that manner that told me I was frightening her. I promised I would not frighten her anymore; that my intent was to verify what I was again experiencing and also to communicate that she was not alone in this world, as she had feared. If I was able to travel astrally to check on her, (while I am still of human form and without her knowing) then it is reasonable to believe that those on the other side can check on us in spirit form (without us knowing).

Ok, wait, now that I'm thinking about it I just realized that my experiences with Claire were not the first time I experienced Astral Travel. Back when I was in college I was living with my roommate's family during the summer break. My roommate had six siblings. Her younger sister had followed in her footsteps and had become a very big fan of Bruce Springsteen. Susan couldn't get enough of "Bruce." Her room was lined with posters of Bruce and she played his music day in and out. Bruce was in town that summer doing a concert. The locals all knew where Bruce hung out in Asbury Park. Susan was out for the night at the Springsteen concert. I had to get to bed early, as I was working as a roofer and had to be at work by 6:30am. While sleeping I astrally traveled to a small smoke-filled bar. I saw Susan and a friend of hers. It was very late when Bruce Springsteen entered the bar. Susan was in her glory and a bundle of nerves. Despite this, she gathered up the courage to introduce herself to Bruce, who was gracious in meeting this teenage fan. When Susan came home that morning (about 5:00am) I heard met her at the stairwell and said: "You met Bruce! I saw you. You met him!" She confirmed this, and with glee said: "I've got the glass he was drinking from!" I knew all the details just like I had been there—because I was.

Of a more personal nature was a 'dream that wasn't a dream' that occurred on August 6, 1983. It was night time, in the early a.m. hours. I was sleeping and dreaming that I was at a playground with my college roommates. We were sitting on a merry-go-round, but it was not in motion. Suddenly, a male presence appeared and addressed me. It was like he was appearing from a tunnel. In fact, everything was a hazy circle, and the noises from the playground were muffled. My roommates were no longer in view. It was just me and this male spirit. In a rather factual manner, he stated: "Uncle Mike is having a heart attack." Don't ask me how, but with that one statement I had a flood of knowledge. I knew that Uncle Mike was having the attack at that very minute, that it was very early in the a.m. hours, and that he was going to die. My whole body jolted with adrenalin, with the intention to quickly wake and attend to the situation at hand. But the male spirit spoke to me again. This time he raised his right hand and with peace in his voice stated: "It's OK." Again, I cannot explain how, but I knew that this meant that I was to remain asleep—that it was not time for me to act yet—that Uncle Mike would be with the Light soon and that my task would be at attend to my Mother and Aunt the next morning. Somehow I knew deep down inside that everything was at it was supposed to be. Uncle Mike would be with the Light, and he knew this, as did this male presence. Now I had this knowledge as well…and that was OK. With that, the male spirit was gone, and I fell into a sound sleep.

My mother awakened me at 6:30 the next morning. "Vickie," she said, "Uncle Mike had a heart attack last night. I need to go to the hospital." She went on to tell me that the hospital stated he arrived there in the early morning hours, and that at that time he requested, very strongly, that no immediate family members be notified until 6:00am that morning. He reportedly did not want anyone awakened before that time, as he did not want to disturb their sleep. I knew that it would be my task to get my mother and my Aunt to the hospital, which was in 'upstate' New York. The drive was long on a good day, but on this day we lost our way. It took twice as long as it normally would, and I knew Uncle Mike would "cross-over" within minutes of our arrival.

This was my Uncle's second heart attack. He had his first at 45 years of age. Five years had passed, and he had just been to his physician's office for a checkup. The physician gave my Uncle a clean bill of health that Friday, stating that the probability of another heart attack was low due to the fact that five years had elapsed. Two days later, my Uncle was dead. I was unable to see my Uncle before he died, as my mother did not want my last memory of him to be a disturbing one. I think Uncle Mike knew what was going on, and hopefully found peace in the fact that everything went as he had requested. I felt close to him in his death. The spirit that came to me provided me with a beautiful experience, for even though I grieve when a loved one dies, I do not fear death. I believe I understand some of what that process is all about. One certainly "dies alone," but there is much help and facilitation in the process. I am grateful to the male spirit. He taught me much about life, as well as the process of death.

## Psychic Pain

*Sometimes I have to stop and ask myself whether what I am experiencing is mine or whether it perhaps belongs to someone else. I have had many occasions where I felt anxious or depressed and wondered where it was coming from, as nothing was going on in my life to cause the feelings. Invariably I find out that it was a friend, family member, or client who was experiencing the feelings or thoughts at the time I experienced them. Sometimes I am able to ask who the experience is in reference to, and then I call them to offer support. Most of the time, information just comes through, like a news bulletin. Sometimes I will send a message back (spiritually that is) inviting (or telling) them to call me. It is not unusual for the phone to ring before the day is out. What I have learned is that we communicate telepathically all the time. It's just a matter of whether we are 'plugged in' or not.*

For approximately four months I had been completing the psychosocial assessments on all the clients admitted to the agency I was working for. I enjoy the assessment process because it's like putting pieces of a puzzle together. Frequently, I can be of service to the client by helping uncover an important issue or by finding a previously undiagnosed problem. It had been months since I had the opportunity to facilitate a group process counseling session. On this one particular day, a coworker was at a workshop and I had the pleasure of facilitating her process group. The group ran from 10:30a.m.-12:00 p.m. There were approximately ten women in the group. All but one or two had histories that were wrought with trauma and pain. During that group I was able to teach the women that one can work on old issues in the present, without providing graphic details of trauma. These women were discovering as a group that their individual issues were the same, if not very similar. The only difference was how they had responded or reacted to the pain. Suddenly, the aloneness of trauma dissipated, and the room began acknowledging the universality of suffering. There is healing in validation and universality. A joyous calm was in the room when the group ended.

As I stood from my chair, I felt a sharp pain at the base of my back. The pain was so sharp that I found it nearly impossible to stand up straight. My first thought was: "Where did this come from?" The immediate thought that followed was: "This is not 'my pain.'" By 'my pain' I am referring to the fact that, historically, when I have back pain it is on my left or right side. The pain feels like a soft tissue strain, resulting from a muscle strain. This current pain felt like it was located in the bone. My pain is muscle-related, not bone-related. I didn't give it much thought, and walked back to my office. About an hour later I noticed that the voice mail indicator on my phone had been activated. The call and message had been placed at approximately 11:30 a.m. that same day (at the time I had been facilitating the group). It was a message from a former client. She had called to tell me that she had just found out that she was having back surgery the next day, and that she needed some emotional support. I phoned her immediately. In the course of our discussion, I asked her where her back pain was. She stated: "At the base of my spine." As it turns out, 'my pain' was actually 'her pain.' Her pain was with me on and off throughout the rest of the day. It completely went away the next day, at the time of her surgery.

A few days later, on a Friday, I found myself thinking of another former client throughout the day. This client had completed treatment approximately a month before. His 'presence' kept coming in and out of my consciousness. My gut instinct told me that he had relapsed and was in trouble. I looked up his phone number and called, only to hear the standard cell phone voice message: "The number that you are trying to reach is not in service at this time." This was not a good sign, and further validation that this person was not doing well. I sent a message to him via the universe, telling him to get back to treatment. I believe my exact words were: "Get your ass back here." I sent that message throughout the weekend. On Monday morning, as I was backing my truck into a parking space, I saw the client's Jeep in the spot next to the one I was backing into. A staff member pulled up in a golf cart to inform me that the client had relapsed and had checked himself in during the early morning hours. He appeared confused when I stated: "I already know." When I saw the client, my statement to him was: "I see you got my message." He wanted to know how I knew. I simply explained that he had told me. This readmission became a pivotal point in this man's recovery. Our paths had crossed three times before. Now it was time to do the work that we were supposed to do together. We worked, one on one, to resolve a secret that had been haunting him throughout life. The secret left him in a paralyzing paradox of living on the fringe of life and death. He didn't feel worthy of living, yet did not want to die. Caught between life and death, his only manner of coping was to numb himself with drugs…leading to an increasingly dysfunctional life. Our task before us, we both dug down deep for the tempestuous path to healing. Together we took the journey from darkness to light.

# CHAPTER THREE

# SPIRITUAL STOPS ALONG THE PATH

*Throughout my life there have been moments of connectedness. Moments where it was obvious to me that there was a Power greater than myself that was working in my life. Moments of wakefulness, where my attention was heightened and I could be conscious of a Higher Source working in my life. These occasions were dotted along my path, as if to remind me that I was not alone on this journey. Some were profound, some simple, each brought with it an invitation for humbleness and reverence from within. I share some of those moments with you.*

## Close Calls
### Road Rage

Thus far in my driving career I have been very fortunate. I believe it would be fair to say that as a driver I tend to be alert, careful, and conscientious. It is equally fair to say that I have had times in my life when I should not have been behind the wheel. Whether I was impaired by alcohol, dissociation (being on "automatic pilot" and not being fully conscious of the act of driving), or rage, I had no business driving. There was a time in my life when I had a problem with road rage. It seemed to me that I was the only one who knew how to drive. Worse yet, I kept getting behind all the idiots out there who got there license at the 'Five and Dime'. I was quick to a self-righteous anger that would manifest in yelling, cursing, giving the finger, and blowing the horn. I was truly a menace on the road, completely out of control. I was inviting trouble, wanting a fight. I was angry. I was right. I was a danger to myself and others, and I didn't care about that at all.

There were the obvious victims who didn't deserve my impatient tirades. Whether they were "having a bad day" with their driving skills, or whether they were just bad drivers, they clearly did not deserve my abuse. I try to make amends to them by practicing patience with others today. I ease up, slow down, and say a little prayer that they get to their destination with safety. There were others on the road like myself, Road-Ragers, waiting for the opportunity to do battle. When the two of us would meet, it would "be on" so to speak. Back in the day, I was in my twenties and driving a 1972 Opel GT. This is a tiny little car that looks like a corvette, and was manufactured from 1968-1974. I would take on Truckers in my little Opel GT. It was not uncommon for me to be run off the road, or to have Truckers hurl missiles at me (rocks, bottles) from their cab. This was not enough to stop my behavior. In fact, I saw it as justification for my rage.

Time went on, and my rage problem seemed to quiet down. I would encounter road rage less frequently, yet it was still there, waiting for the opportunity to emerge. I was still in my twenties, and now driving an Oldsmobile. It was evening, and I was coming home from an extended day at work. I was tired and "just wanted to get home." Someone in front of me did "something stupid" and I went off. I remember yelling and giving him the finger. We came to a stop at a traffic light, and as I glanced over at him I saw a look in his eyes that was not the customary return rage that I was used to seeing. What I encountered was a hunter's stare, a look of controlled madness. At that precise moment that our eyes met, he flashed his gun. I felt a cold chill, and knew I was in trouble. I knew I needed to get away from danger. It all happened so quickly. He flashed the gun, the light changed, and I hit the accelerator. I was confident in my driving skills because, after all, I was from Long Island—the greatest training ground on earth. Well, he may have been as well. I went into a neighborhood that was easy to get lost in if you didn't know where you were going. Despite my twists and turns, he kept up with me. The hunt went on for a good 15-20 minutes before I was convinced that I had lost him. My heart was pounding and I was in a cold sweat. I knew that I had narrowly escaped injury or death. I also knew in that instant that this was not a game. This was not about righteousness, as the ego has no defense against a loaded gun. Life was so much more powerful than my pitiful ego. It all became crystal clear, in every cell of my being. That incident occurred nearly fifteen years ago, and since that dark evening I have not had one incident of road rage. In fact, it is rare when I get angry while driving. When I encounter potential Road-Ragers it is a reminder of who I was on the road. Instead of engaging, I stay focused on my driving, let them carry on, and wish them well as they pass by me. This was a close call that required a shift in my thinking in order to generate a profound change. I am grateful for the lesson.

## 360°

There have been two very close calls with regard to accidents that I have encountered in my life. Both of these incidents were totally out of my control, and the outcome was the same. One occasion occurred on a return trip from college during semester break. I was driving from Long Island, where my parents' home was, to central New York. I made a stop in Westchester to pick up my roommate. It was the dead of winter and we did not know it but we were heading into a blizzard. I was driving that tiny little Opel GT. The roads into central New York cut through the mountains (we called them hills). It is common for the roads to develop a slick sheet of ice, and it can be very treacherous. The trip started with a cold rain, then sleet, and then a driving snow. About 2/3 of the way into our trip it was getting clear that we may have to stop for the night, as the visibility was getting less and less. We were just coming up over the top of a very steep "hill," when the Opel started to go into skid. I turned into the skid, as I had many times before. Instead of coming to a stop, we went into a 360° spin down the mountainside. There was no time to think, nothing to do, I was rendered completely powerless. In the flash of that instant, instead of tensing with panic, I just relaxed. I was conscious of just letting go and feeling washed over with a sense of peace. I was prepared to die, and completely surrendered to that reality. In the process of spinning I saw we were headed for the median and cars were coming along the highway in the opposite direction. I waited for impact. It all happened within seconds, yet it was strangely in slow motion, almost as if time had lost its concept and we were in suspended animation.

The car came to rest. I turned to my roommate and asked: "Are you ok?" She looked at me like I was crazy. I mean, exactly what does that mean? She just saw her life flash before her eyes and I wanted to know if she was "ok"? When I asked her if she was hurt, she was able to communicate that she was unharmed; and was able to respond to me without the initial glare that I had received. We got out of the car and walked around. There was a small dent in the front end, but nothing serious. Strangely, no one stopped to see if we needed assistance. In fact, there was no one around. We were alone, in a time before cell phones even existed. The Opel had come to a rest in the median, a few feet from the road. It was facing in the correct direction of traffic, yet b/c of the snow I knew I couldn't drive back onto the road. We were in the middle of a blizzard, without any form of communication, and in need of a tow truck. We may have survived the spin down the mountainside, but now hypothermia was going to become a real concern. Don't ask me how, but somehow we managed to lift the car back onto the road. Even more of a surprise was that my little Opel started up when I turned the key. We got in the car, traveled to the next exit and safely arrived at a hotel. We were both awestruck at what had just happened, and discussed our experience throughout the night. We each approached the spin differently, me with a complete release and peaceful surrender, and her with shear panic and rigid brace for impact. We both came out of the experience with a strong conviction that nothing but Divine Intervention had kept us out of harm's way.

Fast forward about five years later, to 1985. My roommate from college (and now partner) and I were now living in Florida. She had just purchased a Suzuki Samurai. They had just come out on the market as one of the first SUVs. Marketed for fun and adventure, their "shelf life" was not long (1985-1995), as they became known in 1988 as an unsafe vehicle due to their tendency to rollover. We were heading north from Fort Lauderdale to visit my parents in Vero Beach. It was a 2 ½ hour ride, and my partner granted me the honor of christening her new vehicle on the open road. About 2/3 into the trip the scene from the mountains seemed to replay itself. It had just started raining, and we were coming up unto a major bridge on the highway. I was conscious of the fact that I was getting boxed in by 2 cars and an 18 wheeler. This always heightens my awareness because it limits options if something unexpected were to occur. I make it a practice to avoid these situations, but on this particular day and at this particular moment it was beyond my control. Suddenly, a car swerved in front of me and I had to swerve to avoid impact.

There was only one option, only one split second to avoid the impact of the car in front of me and the 18 wheeler beside me. I recall hearing a horn and feeling that oh too familiar 360° spin. Again, it was common sense that impact was going to occur. Again, there was absolutely nothing I could do. In fact, the odds of catastrophic impact were high. Again, without conscious thought, I relaxed. I felt that peace again and just surrendered. I don't know how many times we spun, but I know that we came to an abrupt stop at the side of the road, facing oncoming traffic. How we didn't rollover is beyond my comprehension, given the speed of the vehicle, the road conditions, and the swerve I had to make to avoid hitting the car in front of me. Again, knowing that I was unharmed I stupidly turned to my partner and said: "Are you ok?" Again, I got that "Are you insane?" glare from her eyes. She was emotionally shook up, but physically unharmed. We were stunned by what had just occurred. There was no logical explanation for why no impact had occurred, why there wasn't a four car pile-up, why we didn't rollover, and why there was not one scratch on her brand new vehicle. No one stopped to see if we needed assistance. In fact, once again, there was not a car in sight. It was as if it never happened, except for the fact that we were shaking from that close encounter, the vehicle had come to rest on the side of the highway, and we were facing oncoming traffic. I handed my partner the key to her Suzuki and made some comment about I wasn't sure if it was a good thing that I was driving both times or a bad thing, and that I didn't blame her if she never got in a car with me again. Let's just say she said she preferred not to drive the remainder of the day.

I know that I had nothing to do with any of these close calls. What were the odds of two 360° spins with the same person in the vehicle, with no injury or substantial damage to either person or vehicle? I mean really, what was that all about? Each time it was clearly not our time to go and not part of our paths to be seriously injured. Each time I was awakened to the reality that something greater than I had intervened. There was this tremendous sense that I was not alone, that I was being watched over. Whether I was placing myself in harm's way with my road rage, or practicing safe driving techniques, I was delivered to safety.

## Guardian Angels

I am an animal lover to the highest degree. Yes, I am 'one of those' that will risk life and limb to save an animal. It does not matter what kind of animal it is. I've stopped along the road to rescue dogs, cats, turtles, pigs, squirrels, cows, raccoons, opossums, birds, snakes, rats, and even butterflies. Yes, butterflies. While driving down the road one day I watched a butterfly get clipped by a truck. In my rearview mirror I saw the butterfly fluttering in the median. My passenger was confused when I pulled over, not having seen the butterfly. I got out of my truck, stopped traffic and picked up the butterfly in the middle of the road. It was still alive, with some damage to one of its wings. I drove home with the butterfly and placed it on a leaf. Within a few minutes it recovered from the shock of its accident and was able to fly off. It was a simple gesture on my part, only requiring a few minutes from my day to make an impact on this small life.

In my many missions to save the life of an animal, I've been honked at, yelled at, and scowled at by passers-by. I just get this tunnel-vision and go into action. I know there are others out there that are just like me. Occasionally we meet up on an impromptu rescue, and thank one another for caring enough to intervene. We are the minority.

## The African American Man

One of my missions occurred on the way home from work. I had just finished my 3pm-11pm shift. It was Saturday night, and I was just coming upon an intersection in town that was in the heart of "the hood." The light turned red, and as I came to a stop my eye caught a small kitten that was at the curb across the street. It was sure death for such a tiny creature to be in such a precarious place. As soon as the light turned green I pulled over to a vacant gas station, near the curb where the kitten was. The kitten saw me and ungraciously darted off between concrete rubble at the gas station. I could hardly see, because it was so late and there were no lights. I was trying desperately to find this little life, calling to it and trying to coax it out from its hiding spot. I was determined to rescue this little one, and 'locked on' my mission. Suddenly, I heard this voice from over my shoulder. From the voice I knew it was an older African American man. He said to me: "Ma'am? Excuse me, Ma'am?" I was too busy to turn and look at him, as I had to find this kitten. Again I heard: "Ma'am? It's not safe for you to be here. You need to leave." There was urgency in his voice that forced me to pay attention to him. As I turned toward him I saw before me a frail elderly man. I wondered what **he** was doing there on the corner in that dark night and wondered how safe **he** was. I said: "Yeah, I know, but I've got to find this kitten first. It's going to die out here." The man now pleaded with me: "It's not safe for you here, Miss. I've been watching across the street. You see those men, they are about to come over here. I shouldn't even be telling you this. You need to leave, now!" In my haste to rescue, and in my blinding focus, I had abandoned all survival instincts and was about to be victimized. Without the intervention of this Guardian Angel, sure harm would have come to me. I humbly thanked him, got in my truck, and quietly left. There is Grace in this world.

### The Man in the Truck

Not all missions were of the animal kind. A friend of mine had an elderly father who had recently been diagnosed with Alzheimer's. She had not had the heart to take his car keys from him, and one day her mother called to say he had left the apartment and not returned. She filed a missing persons report and a bunch of us drove around in search of his car. There are many canals in south Florida, and it is not uncommon for the impaired or the elderly to end up in these canals. Days went by and finally she got a call from a hospital in a remote town in northern Florida. It was during a time when wild fires were out of control and major highways were being shut down. Apparently her father had come to an area that was being detoured due to the fires and a trooper noticed that he was not oriented. We set out to go pick up her father, who was safe and unharmed at a hospital.

The hospital was located in a very rural area. We were detoured several times and finally got 'within range' of the hospital but were clearly lost. We stopped at a gas station, and one of our 'rescue crew' went in to get directions. A man pulled up in a truck and approached us. He asked if we were lost and needed directions. We explained out plight and our goal of getting to the hospital. This man said he could 'get us there in thirty minutes' using back roads that only the locals new about—otherwise it could take 'an hour or two' to get there. We were a bit skeptical. Who was this guy? How did he just appear from out of nowhere? Why did he want to help? We asked if he was heading that way, and he said that he was actually heading in the opposite direction, but that he would escort us. He warned that we would have to stay close, as we could be in harm's way by the locals or the sheriffs if we did not. We got in the car and wondered if we were now about to follow a serial killer. We outnumbered him, but were clearly at his mercy with regard to where he was taking us. We turned down many dirt roads, and approximately thirty minutes later came to a crossroad where several new buildings were located. There was a small sign that indicated we were at the hospital. Almost in unison we all turned to wave at the driver to thank him. The truck had just vanished, with no sign of a dust trail. It was as if he had been a figment of our imagination. There was a profound silence in the car, and when the silence broke we all quietly wondered if an Angel had not escorted us.

It turned out that the area was even more remote than we had anticipated. Apparently the folks in this town grew up in that town and never left. We were asking for I95, a well traveled, major artery in Florida. There was no one in the hospital who had ever heard of I95!! Ok, there was one, but she didn't know how to get to it. She was able to call someone and get some very rough directions that got us to another roadblock that got us to a state trooper that got us to I95. It was another validation that there is a Higher Order to things and that I am just a traveler in this journey of life.

# CHAPTER FOUR

# COMING FULL CIRCLE

*I've had moments in life when I've been "on top" and moments in life when I've been "on the bottom." A brief example would be when I was in high school. In the afternoon I was an athlete on the team. I was popular because I was the best. I felt accepted and admired, and my peers looked upon me as a leader. By day, in gym class, these very same peers would make fun of me and I would frequently be chosen last when the gym teacher would tell us to 'pick teams.' I was picked on unmercifully during school hours yet respected on the athletic field.*

*There have been moments in my life when it seemed like I was in a time warp, as such, where I suddenly realized that life had come full circle with me. These were humbling moments that made me keenly aware that I was not in charge, that there was a Higher Order to things, and that God has an incredibly wonderful sense of humor—oft used at my expense and to teach me a lesson.*

## Food Stamps

My first career-oriented job was working at Covenant House-FL, which is a runaway shelter for young adults 21 years of age and younger. I was initially hired as an "Intake Youth Specialist" which meant I admitted clients to the facility. I was quickly promoted and eventually became a supervisor on the floor that housed 18-21 year old males. I was 23 years old, and I probably looked younger than some of our clients. I was fresh out of college, with a hard work ethic and ideals that in no way came close to reality. I questioned everything and saw ways to make things more organized and efficient. My role as supervisor put me in a position of authority over people much older than myself, with far more experience in the field. I was respected for my ability and my potential, but certainly not for my wisdom or experience (I had none). I had not learned the art of delegation and would typically overextend myself. By the time I resigned from this job I was "burned out" (A term that is used to describe one who is physically, mentally, emotionally, and spiritually depleted as a result of being overworked, underpaid, underappreciated, and disillusioned by the helping profession.) In short, I was not a happy camper and I was not fun to be around. My resignation came shortly after I was called to a meeting with my supervisors. I remember that their tone was initially one of concern for me, that I felt placated (why was I being a target of focus when my immediate supervisor was so burned out that I found him in a maintenance room, literally standing in the corner facing the wall—in the dark), and wasn't going to tolerate such a double standard. My resignation came in the form of an extended middle finger. (They let me stay to finish out my two weeks, and I actually left on good terms).

My next position was as a substance abuse counselor, working for the county. I thought I was hired on my credentials. My supervisor later confided in me that I was called in for an interview because on my resume I had noted that while in New York I had been a commercial roofer and had also worked in Harlem as a construction laborer. She assumed that I was African American, and since the county had encouraged her to hire an African American, she immediately called me for an interview. That's how I got in the door. What probably got me the job was that I was in recovery and had been abstinent from all mind/mood altering substances for five years. At that time, in order to be a substance abuse counselor the only requirement was that you were in recovery. Believe it or not, a Bachelor's degree was not a requirement and there was no mandatory certification or license by the State.

Anyway, I worked for the county as a counselor in the residential and outpatient programs. The experience was fertile training ground and proved to be just what I needed with regard to my grooming as a professional. I learned about "systems" there, and was counseled by my peers to maintain my ideals but not expect them to materialize. One of the greatest coping tools that was offered to me was the phrase: "Common sense will not be tolerated." This was the answer that my colleague would utter when I would start in with one of my "why" questions during a staff meeting. That one phrase answered all my questions and helped me to surrender to the fact that I was powerless over this system. I remained a county employee for about 6 years and then my own mental illness forced me to resign. I had always had problems with depression. In fact, the onset of my depression was at about seven years of age. I had been suicidal since about 13 years of age. The depression just got worse over the years and I went from therapist to therapist to try to find someone who could help me. I finally did, and my diagnoses went from depression to Post Traumatic Stress Disorder to Dissociative Identity Disorder. I won't go into detail here, but just suffice it to say that the diagnosis matched. I was now in a time of my life when I found it increasingly difficult to function. It was as if the walls were falling down all around me. I knew that ethically I could not continue in my role as a helper, when I was clearly the one needing help. I had come full circle.

I entered a nine month period of unemployment. During that time I had intensive therapy. For the first time in my life I had to accept government assistance. Signing up for unemployment was embarrassing to me. I didn't want to accept help, but knew that I needed that help in order to survive. The money I received was enough to pay for rent, utilities, gas for my truck, and my truck payment. There was not much money left after those bills were paid. For a few months I existed on $12 a week for food. I pretty much existed on eggs and noodles, milk, and corn pancakes. Not surprisingly, I lost quite a bit of weight. It became clear to me that I was in need of more government assistance. I felt utterly ashamed when I walked into the Food Stamp office. The workers behind the glass were not very friendly. They didn't smile and somehow seemed to think that I knew the routine. I did not, and felt lost. I wanted to leave—no I wanted to run screaming from the building. I wanted to explain to someone my unique set of circumstances, that I wasn't someone who takes advantage of the system, that I was educated and was a "helping professional."

There is no room for pride at the food stamp office. You just get in line. I waited for what seemed like an eternity going from one waiting area to another. I finally made it to the inside administrative waiting area, where I was told to wait yet again, and that a counselor would be there to help me. A man walked past me and paused. He turned toward me and greeted me by name. I was so stunned and so shame-based and couldn't believe that I would meet someone who knew me at the Food Stamp Office. Not only did this man know me, but he had been someone that I supervised while I worked at Covenant House. He was initially happy to see me. With a smile on his face, he asked if I was applying for a position or if I was there with a client. I told the truth. I told him I was there trying to get on Food Stamps. The smile vaporized from his face and he made some sort of apology, excused himself, and disappeared down the hall. I never saw him again—ever.

God and I had a serious talk at that moment. It went something like this: "What was that all about? You think that's funny, don't you. Well, I'm not laughing. Why were we supposed to see each other here today? He's not my 'counselor', but he easily could have been assigned to me. So why did we even have to see each other. I didn't even notice him, why did he have to notice me?" Suddenly I was not feeling ashamed, but humbled. I recognized that job titles meant nothing. I inherently understood that we are all human and vulnerable to changes in life that are beyond our control. I intuitively knew that it was more important to treat all people with dignity and respect, because you don't know where they came from or where they are going. I learned that it was important not to make assumptions. In that moment I embraced the fact that it was not about carrying shame. It was about holding my head up, knowing that I was not alone, and that I just had to do whatever it took to survive. Pride aside, I was free to do just that.

## Another Cosmic Joke

I survived food stamps and unemployment. I was living at a level of poverty that I never imagined I would experience. I had over ten years of sobriety, had a bachelor's degree, had worked as a substance abuse counselor and was living in the heart of "crack town" in an efficiency apartment where prostitutes and drug dealers were regularly doing business in my driveway.

Fortunately for me, I had a very knowledgeable therapist who was able to properly diagnose and provide treatment for me. After a lifetime (literally) of well-intentioned therapists, psychologists, and psychiatrists the universe was gracious enough to place me in the care of this gifted healer. Our work together was intensive and I am eternally grateful that she had the patience and insight to see me through. The treatment was successful, which meant that I integrated. From dozens of split personalities, I became one. You'd think I would have been relieved, delighted, happy, or maybe even grateful. Instead, I went into a period of grieving. I didn't know how I would manage on my own. My therapist was telling me that it was time to rejoin life, to go back to work, and to do the work that I was meant to do. I was afraid. I didn't want to join life. Now, more than ever, I wanted this life to be over. I wanted to go back Home. I hated this earthly plane and wanted out. I wanted to go Home. Life was just too difficult and obviously God had made a mistake when I was sent here. I'm not cut out for a human experience.

I had suicidal ideation since the age of thirteen. I had sat on the ledge of the tallest dorm in college, while drunk, with every intention of leaping to my death—until I realized I had an audience and climbed back in the window. Later in life I had a loaded gun that I would hold to my head and in my mouth, trying desperately to get up the nerve to pull the trigger—fearful that I would screw it up and be in a vegetative state or a paraplegic the rest of my life. I wanted to die, on and off, for about fifteen years. I lived in survival mode. I didn't enjoy life. Now, I was "cured" and didn't know what for. What was the point, if I was still going to struggle and be miserable?

One evening in November of 1991, I was feeling particularly depressed and alone. I tried calling a couple people and even tried attending a 12 Step Meeting, but nothing was alleviating my distress. In fact my despair continued to build as the evening progressed. I don't know why, but at some point in that evening I decided I wasn't going to hang in there anymore. I wanted out. A suicide attempt is an impulsive, completely selfish act. I thought about no one but myself. I didn't even think about my cats— important things like how long it would take to find my body, how the cats would survive, or even who would take care of them for the rest of their lives. I didn't think about how this would impact my therapist, my friends, and my family. I didn't think at all, I just acted. I went to my medication and began to calculate how much I would need to take in order to die. I knew that if I took too much I would likely become nauseas, vomit, and fail in my attempt. It had to be enough to render me unconscious quickly enough to bypass vomiting and then cause death. I took the pills and went to bed.

It was probably four or five in the morning when I became conscious. I don't know if I opened my eyes. It seems unimportant, as the only thing that I was conscious of was that I was alive. I was almost between death and life. I felt like I was floating, yet everything felt very heavy and black at the same time. I instinctively knew I was in trouble, yet didn't have the presence of mind to even care. It was almost like being in suspended animation—a moment of complete nothingness. Then I simultaneously heard Hanna, my spirit guide, and felt Shannon, my angel. Hanna said in a quiet whisper: "Just keep breathing and we'll do the rest." Despite my compromised state of being, I knew that this meant two things. First, it meant that I was in danger and that I had to do my part in remaining alive. Breathing is an involuntary act. We don't think about breathing, it just happens. What I was being told was that I was going to have to volunteer to breathe. I was going to have to choose to take in air in order to survive. This meant that with each breath I would be making a conscious decision to choose to live. In other words, it was up to me whether I was to live or die. Second, it meant that I was not alone and that they would be actively doing their part to make sure I survived—if I chose to survive. It didn't matter what "the rest" was that they needed to do. I trusted that they would do it. I chose to breathe, and with that choice made a decision to be a part of life. I have not had suicidal thoughts since then. I have been depressed, even wanted to go Home, but not wanted to take my own life. In fact, since making a decision to be a part of life I have been free to actually enjoy life. My depression is more in remission than out of remission, and it is more manageable when it does rear its ugly head. The key was in choosing life.

A couple hours later it became clear to me that I needed help. Breathing was requiring a concerted effort. My cats were in distress, approaching me in a helpless manner and looking at me with fear. I called the therapist on call (my therapist was on a cruise) and irrationally thought that she would talk me through this. She wisely called 911. I told the ambulance crew that I had mistakenly taken too much of my medication—that I was having trouble sleeping and took a little too much. I don't think they bought it. Next thing I know I was on the stretcher and on my way to the ER. The Docs and Nurses in the ER were not very friendly. In fact, they seemed angry with me. They asked what happened and I told them the same story—that I mistakenly took too much of my medication. The ER Doc ordered some charcoal solution and I was told that if I didn't cooperate they would insert a tube down my nose and into my stomach in order to administer it. I asked a male nurse why everyone was so angry. He almost whispered: "Because we are in the business of saving lives and we don't take too kindly to someone who is trying to end their life." I lied yet again, telling him it was all a mistake. He kindly shook his head back and forth and said: "You took six times the lethal dose. You knew exactly what you were doing. We don't even know how you're alive at this point. We can't even pump your stomach because too much time has gone by. All we can do is administer this charcoal to absorb the medication. Don't give them (the docs) a hard time or they will make it harder on you." There was nothing to argue. I cooperated and concentrated on getting released.

It was not long before the ER physician returned. He advised me that he had Baker Acted me for involuntary hospitalization. He said he didn't believe my story about not being able to sleep and believed I was at high risk of another suicide attempt. Now I was in a full fledge panic. I tried to reason with this man, reassure him that I was not suicidal, that I was under the care of a therapist—all to no avail. I was going, the papers had been signed and there was no discussion. I figured I was going to the psych unit in the hospital. I didn't want to go there, but knew that there was no arguing at this point. Best thing to do was act as if this was all just a big misunderstanding.

Two men came for me for "transport." Transport? I asked why I needed two men and where I was getting transported to. The answer stunned me. I had been Baker Acted to South Florida State Hospital and they were there to take me in a non-emergency ambulance—a 40 minute drive. The state hospital was where really truly crazy people went. Talk about an 'Eminence Front', I continued to act as though this was all a big mistake. Even the ambulance crew remarked that I seemed fine to them. They even thought I might get released as soon as I got to admitting at the State Hospital. I figured they ought to know, as they saw really crazy people every day. Well, guess what, they were wrong. The Baker Act is a mandatory minimum 72 hour holding period—and it's up to a psychiatrist to determine if you are of danger to self or others.

I was now a patient at South Florida State Hospital, complete with locked steel doors and bars on the windows. Razor barbed fencing surrounded the hospital grounds. There was clearly no escape. I barely had any clothes on, as I was transported from my apartment in boxer shorts and a t-shirt—not even socks or shoes. (The male ER nurse at the hospital showed me some compassion and gave me a pair of the surgical booties that they wear over their shoes.) They keep the temperature in the State Hospital very low, and it wasn't long before I was shaking from cold. I asked for a blanket and I was told that blankets were not allowed to be "worn." They could only be used during bedtime, and since I was not allowed in my room I could not have a blanket. I explained that I was cold, and I was given an expression from the hospital workers like I was somehow inconveniencing them.

Hours went by and one of the workers called out for me and told me that she was taking me to the 'clothing room.' I figured I could get a sweatshirt and sweatpants. She started holding up dresses and skirts for me to try on. I don't wear dresses or skirts. I refused to wear them since 6th grade and wasn't about to change. This woman was not happy with me, and tried to tell me that I would look nice in a dress. I refused. I think I was handed a dirty sweater, with disdain. I didn't care. I wasn't going to put a dress on for her or anyone else. Besides, how would a dress keep me warm—it was freezing in there!

The patients were not in touch with reality. Most of them were actively psychotic or heavily medicated. It was scary being around them. I tried to 'be invisible' and just stay to myself. Of course, to the hospital attendants this meant that I was isolating. How does one socialize with a "peer" who is hallucinating? I kept my distance—from both patients and staff. It became very clear to me that I was not crazy. All my life I thought I was crazy. I wanted to die, I had many personalities—I must be crazy. Yet, let me tell you, spend some time in a State Hospital and you will know what crazy is. I was in the wrong place. I didn't belong here. In the bathroom there were feces smeared all over the wall. The shower was full of black mold. Patients were inclined to start screaming at a moment's notice. Attendants would come running to subdue and restrain. I felt like I was being punished, punished by the ER physician, by life, by God. In reality I knew I had punished myself.

That first night was very frightening, as the screams would continue throughout the night. I was afraid that I would be attacked—by a patient or attendant—while sleeping and hardly slept as a result. In the morning, when they herded us together for breakfast I was aghast at what they served. It smelled rancid and while I couldn't believe it, it was actually worse than the slop they served in the jail. There was no way I was going to eat that crap. One of the patients, in a moment of clarity, leaned over to me and whispered: "They are always watching you. If you don't eat, they will keep you here longer." I heeded the warning and moved things around on the plate to make it look like I ate. At the end of the meal the attendant made some comment to me about 'not eating much' and I said I had tried and wasn't very hungry.

I was relieved to hear that the psychiatrist was going to meet with me. It wasn't quite 24 hours since my admission and I was looking forward to placating and getting the hell out of there. The psychiatrist's office was small and dimly lit, and there was a female nurse present during the "evaluation." I thought that all I had to do was demonstrate that I was sane and not in danger of hurting self or others. I stuck with my original story ("It's my story and I'm sticking to it") thinking that this was the way to go. The psychiatrist was not buying my story any more that the ER physician had. This psychiatrist was rambling on and I wasn't listening to a word he was saying, because it was beginning to dawn on me that he had no intention of releasing me. I think I interrupted him and asked him if he was going to release me, and I recall this look from him like I was out of my mind. Rage coursed through every blood vessel in my body and I shot out of my chair screaming FUCK YOU and walked out of the office, slamming the door behind me. Now, that was truly a demonstration of sanity and personal control, wasn't it?

I was enraged as much as I was afraid. I was really beginning to wonder **if** I was going to get out. I was completely powerless over my own freedom. I was at the mercy of a psychiatrist, a man, to release me. Surely, there must be a legal way to appeal. Who would listen to me? God knows what they had diagnosed me with. I looked out of the barred windows, feeling like a prisoner. I thought about innocent people who are found guilty of crimes and serve years in our prisons. I thought of prisoners of war in other countries. I thought of other souls who had a plight much more painful and despairing than mine. I now had a real appreciation for the gift of freedom; a freedom that by an impulsive, selfish act, I had given up. We are so fortunate in this country to be born with the right of liberty and freedom. I was humbled and decided to make the best of this current situation, regardless of how repulsive it was.

Somewhere in the 72 hour mark I was again summoned to the psychiatrist's office. I promised myself that no matter what, I would behave myself. It was a different psychiatrist this time, and a different assistant. I was shocked at what transpired. I was all ready to admit to the suicide attempt and to assure the psychiatrist that I now wanted to live. Instead, he started out by advising me that he was very concerned about my sexual orientation. He said that the staff knew that I was a lesbian; that they had tried to get me to wear female clothing (a dress or skirt), and that I had not responded to their direction. He went on to state that I would be depressed and unfulfilled for the remainder of my life if I remained a lesbian. I looked over at the nurse assisting him to see if she was as shocked by this as I was. I got a blank stare.

This was 1991, for crying out loud! Homosexuality was no longer considered a mental illness. It had been removed from the Diagnostic and Statistic Manual's 3rd edition. We had evolved well beyond this! What kind of hellhole was I in?!! I took a deep breath, and much to my utter amazement I launched into the Oscar performance of a lifetime. I asked the good doctor for advice. He said to me that I needed to wear skirts and dresses, start dating men, get married and have children. With the best acting I could muster, I humbly thanked him for his advice. He then said that if I promised to do those things, he would release me. It was all so very clear—at least to him. I was certifiably insane because I was a lesbian. If I promised to change my ways and be a heterosexual then I would become sane and be released from the State Hospital. It was just that simple. I continued with my academy award winning performance.

Since 'common sense would not be tolerated' I decided to join the insanity. I totally surrendered to the insanity of the moment, and promised this man that I would get married and have children. Of course, I had no intention of doing any of the things he made me promise. That didn't matter. This was not a time for idealism. It was about doing what I needed to do to get out of there. Having done that, I was pronounced sane and released from confinement.

So, where's the cosmic joke? Are you ready for this? Years later I was working back at the county as the supervisor of the substance abuse residential program. There were funding crises and shifts in power throughout the county and it was decided to officially close South Florida State Hospital in favor of privatization. This meant that the county workers at the State Hospital had to be absorbed in other county positions or they would be out of work. Guess where many of those county workers were assigned? Yep, where I was now a supervisor. I was now responsible for supervising the very attendants that had monitored me. When a meeting was called to officially meet with our new psychiatrist, my jaw dropped to the floor when I saw that very first psychiatrist that I bellowed "Fuck You" at. By the grace of God, none of them remembered me. Years had passed and I wasn't that impressive or that important to remember—and thank God for that. It wasn't about them, anyway. It was about me and God's little chuckle. Yeah, I had come full circle—and now I was on the other side. "Just keep breathing and we'll do the rest." Gee, thanks.

## _My Calling_

As I've mentioned before, throughout my life I have taken breaks from my profession and worked as a manual laborer. I've been a commercial roofer, a construction laborer, a lawn maintenance/landscape laborer, and a roofing estimator. I've also worked on a road crew laying asphalt, and painted homes—inside and out. Manual labor helps me to clear my mind and literally work through depression. It empowers me physically, mentally, and spiritually. I feel like I am in harmony with nature when I am working physically. During periods of burn out, I return to manual labor to sometimes literally dig my way through my vortex (or as Shirley MacLaine would say: my "desert period").

On one such occasion, I was working in Fort Lauderdale as a roofing estimator. It was six months before Hurricane Andrew hit. The owner of the company initially trained me as a sales representative. I enjoyed that, but the problem was that what I enjoyed was educating people about roofs. When it came to "closing the sale" I was not very good. My company's prices were higher than others, and I just didn't have that competitive edge to manipulate people into investing in our services. I made sales, but not enough. The owner saw my work ethic and organizational skills and decided to train me to estimate roofs. The salesmen were not meticulous enough with their estimates and it was costing him money.

I loved being on a roof. There's nothing like sitting on the top of a roof and looking out over the horizon. It's so incredibly peaceful. You can just sit there and watch the world whirl. Of course, I didn't sit for long, but I would always take a moment to stand there and just breathe in the tranquility. On occasion I would be called to measure a roof with a very steep pitch. From the driveway most roofs look pretty tame and easy to walk on. The steep ones can be very deceptive, and once you actually climb up there it can make the sweat pour out of you. On more than one occasion I preferred to just scooch around on my butt—there was no way I was going to stand and risk falling victim to gravitational pull. I got my measurements and got the hell out of there—hoping nobody had watched me in the process. Thankfully, that rarely happened. Most of the time I was so comfortable up there that I had to remind myself I was on a roof—lest I step off the edge in a moment of complacency.

Whenever I'm in the manual trades I have this uneasy feeling that I am doing something that I am not supposed to be doing. Almost as if I am on vacation from my calling and that God is entertaining this in order to appease me. However, I definitely have that feeling that I am on a strict time limit and that I need to understand that I will be returning to my profession—on God's time and not mine.

I had just finished taking measurements on a roof and began to descend the ladder. An elderly woman came out of the house and started asking me questions about the roof. I sat down with her with the intention of educating her about the products and services she would be receiving. Instead, she began to tell me her life story. It's as if she sat down and someone pushed the "play" button. She told me that she had been a survivor of the holocaust, and went into detail about her experience in a concentration camp. She showed me the tattoo she was given, discussed her liberation, and how she arrived in the United States and married and had a child. She was not finished, yet stopped abruptly, almost as if awakening from an altered state. She apologized to me, and said: "I am so sorry. I don't know what happened. I have never told my story to anyone before. I don't know why this happened." I placed my hand on hers and said: "It's OK. I know why. You needed to tell. Your story is safe with me." I went on to reassure her that I had been a counselor most of my life and that I was accustomed to witnessing people's pain and trauma. I made sure she was OK and left her home knowing that my time as a roofing estimator was running out. A few days later I heard from the elderly woman's daughter. She called to thank me and also to apologize that her mother had taken up so much of my time. She said that her mother had never discussed the details of the holocaust, and was shocked that she told me her story. I found it sad that both the mother and daughter felt a need to apologize to me. I felt that an honor had been bestowed upon me that few can experience in this lifetime, for this woman gave me a gift of vulnerability and trust. I was so honored to have been able to just bear witness to her trauma. I knew that a Higher Power was with us, that time stood still that summer afternoon, and prayed that her courage to speak her truth made way for the Light of Peace to wash over her soul.

I left my job as a roofing estimator right after Hurricane Andrew hit. My colleagues were alive with the prospect of making money. I saw greed in their eyes, and I knew it was time to move on. They said I was crazy—that I could name a price and people were signing in desperation without question. I understood that people were desperate and refused to be a part of the opportunistic frenzy. Time was up. I had departed from my calling and it was time to return.

# CHAPTER FIVE

# DO NOT DEPART

There have been many experiences throughout my career that have made a lasting impression on me. One of the more profound experiences occurred in the late 1990's. My partner at the time was working at a hospital assessing patients on a crisis stabilization unit. I was working for a nonprofit private mental health center. My partner would frequently talk about a psychiatrist on the unit, whom she admired and respected. This particular psychiatrist was apparently very intelligent, skilled, and knowledgeable. She had a gift when it came to prescribing medications. She was also a bit eccentric and apparently kept to herself quite a bit. My partner found a commonality, as they both enjoyed running (the psychiatrist would literally run marathons 'for fun'). I would hear of their conversations, and each time she mentioned "Christine" I had an image of an Indian woman. Not a Native American "Indian," but a woman from India. It is not uncommon for me to get an image of people when I am talking to them on the phone for the first time, or when I hear about someone in casual conversation. The image is usually very close to reality when I actually meet the person face to face.

My partner talked about Christine with an energy and enthusiasm that I had never seen her display. She would smile at Christine's eccentricities, and also discussed what appeared to be a social phobia that Christine had.

My partner wanted me to meet Christine and, after months of talking about it, a date was set for dinner. I was warned about Christine's anxiety. It wasn't warning enough. Christine was so anxious that I could focus on nothing else but her anxious energy. I could not imagine what my partner saw in her that was so exciting. Christine's partner, on the other hand, was easy to like. In fact, I clicked instantly with her. We had similar interests. She had a calm presence, and was very easy to talk to. The dinner went well only because I liked Christine's partner. When a second dinner was arranged I told my partner of my discomfort with Christine. She assured me that I would like Christine when I got to know her. I had my doubts, but agreed to try again. It was worse than the first time. It seemed to me that Christine was so anxious it was not only impossible to get to know her, but her energy caused an agitation within me. I communicated this with my partner, informing her of my doubts that I would ever see in Christine what she saw.

When the third dinner date was set, I informed my partner that this was my final attempt. I enjoyed the company of Christine's partner, but it just wasn't worth the anxiety that Christine projected. I explained that I was fully supportive of them socializing and becoming friends—without my involvement. Then the strangest thing happened. When Christine came in, she had a CD that she gave us as a gift. She said it was a new jazz CD, and hoped we would like it. I enjoy jazz, yet never pursued an active interest in getting familiar with specific artists. As soon as the CD began to play, there was a peace and tranquility that washed over me. Rick Braun was a musician that I had never heard of, and the music from his *Beat Street* CD was so incredibly soothing to my soul. Suddenly Christine and I had something in common. The anxiety lifted from her, and I saw her aura soften and glow. She had an incredibly warm heart and a wonderful sense of humor. Her intellect was stimulating. I not only enjoyed her company, but knew I could learn from her expertise in psychiatry. Now, instead of feeling repelled from her, I felt drawn to her.

We all went to a Mexican restaurant that evening. I felt so comfortable with Christine that I decided to confide in her about my first image of her. I explained that I typically know what a person looks like before I meet them, and that this time I had been way off. Christine was as white as they come, and clearly American. She was certainly not the woman from India that I had envisioned. As I started explaining this, Christine's eyes got wider and wider. She explained that her father had ministered throughout the world, and that she had spent quite a bit of time as a child growing up in India. The hair stood on the back of my neck and I felt a tingling sensation down my spine. This seemed more than just a coincidence to me.

Dinner that evening was a joy, and we all decided that we wanted to develop a close friendship. We made plans to attend a professional women's basketball game in Orlando, plans to go to Disney together, plans to canoe the Peace River. All this was to occur within the coming weeks. I looked forward in anticipation of the fun we would have, and felt a close connection to both of my new-found friends.

A week or so later my partner and I were in bed for the night, getting ready to turn out the lights. I was struggling to stay awake. We had just finished watching a weekly TV drama, and the news was now coming on. I couldn't stay awake any longer. As I rolled over, I heard there was some "breaking news". I heard the announcer report that a shooting had occurred in a hospital in Miami, and that a psychiatrist had been killed. I made some off the cuff comment about how 'he probably pissed the patient off.' I was thinking, rather judgmentally, that the psychiatrist was probably one of those incompetent doctors that had it coming to him. Not that I was happy someone was killed—it just wasn't a surprise. I had an image of an Indian man, and figured that the patient was upset, didn't understand him, and shot him to death. With that, I was sound asleep.

I was sitting in my supervisor's office the next morning, waiting for the morning staff meeting. As staff filtered in, I heard a buzz about the psychiatrist who had been killed the night before. I had completely forgotten about the incident. I started making irreverent jokes about how "these things happen." I was making one comment after another, attempting to make light of a very serious thing. My supervisor said that Dr. Smith had also been affiliated with our agency and had apparently been loved by the patients. She said "Dr. Smith" a few times before it hit me. I exclaimed: "Hey, wait a minute. I know a Dr. Smith." Shock blanketed me in an instant, as I began to ask questions. I turned to my supervisor and said: "Was this a man or a woman?" "What was her first name?" It all started to register. A horrifying feeling started to overwhelm me, as I humbly said: "Christine

Smith? I think I know who that is. I know a Christine Smith. Dr. Christine Smith? Oh my God. There must be some mistake. This can't be. I need to find a paper. I need to make some phone calls."

I was handed a paper by a colleague and left the office. I read through the article as I walked down the hall to my office. My mind was still desperately trying to hang on to denial. The newspaper said the murdered psychiatrist was a Christine G. Smith. I thought to myself: "Maybe her middle name didn't begin with a G." It was possible that it wasn't her. I called my partner, and asked her if she knew Chris' middle initial. When she stated that she thought it was "G" I felt the blood drain from my head. Nausea and dizziness quickly set in, as I attempted to gently explain to my partner that it was Christine that had been murdered the night before. We made plans to meet and to determine what to do from there. I went to my Program Director, explained the situation, and excused myself. As I was driving home the shock lifted and the brutal reality hit me in the chest. I wailed in grief. I now know what a primal scream sounds and feels like. The pain was coming from deep within and was rushing out in a fury. I was fully present, yet I almost felt like I was observing my process. I rarely raise my voice. I am frequently accused of having no emotion, as I do not react to situations in an intense manner. Yet, here I was screaming, crying, pleading in vain for this all to be a horrible mistake. Grief-stricken was a term that heretofore had no meaning to me. Now I know why the term exists, as I was struck by grief—it didn't just wash over me. When the crying finally subsided, I felt hollow inside.

This incident hit me on more than one level. I had just opened my heart, my soul, to this incredibly wonderful person. I felt connected. She was a spirit of the light. She was one of few that I let in. And just like that, she was gone. News reports provided details of the incident. Apparently a patient on the unit, who was psychotic and a danger to himself and others, approached Christine and asked her to release him from the hospital. This was not her patient; she was just making rounds that night. She informed him that she would not release him. With that, the patient went back to his room, got a gun from his bag, returned to the nurse's station, and shot Dr. Smith in the chest at point blank range. She never had a chance at survival.

The loss of a friend was traumatizing enough. The other issue was that it was a patient that killed her. In my profession, we all know that we put our lives at risk on a daily basis because of the population we work with. We know that. We know it "only takes one." Yet we do what we do, despite the potential danger, because we are called to do it. You just don't think about the danger, even when confronting someone. You do what you have to do in order to assist that person in their process. For the first time in my life, I had to think if it was really worth the risk. What was it all for, anyway? My impact on a person is so small in the larger scheme of things. Was it really worth dying for? The places that I work are not secure. Not in the least. It's like sitting on a golf course, with club in hand during an electric storm, and figuring that the odds are you won't be struck. How long before it was my turn to be hit? My luck is not that good. Suddenly my immortality was gone. It was ripped from me. I was contemplating leaving my profession. I wasn't just thinking about leaving my profession. I was thinking about it seriously enough to be discussing it with others. The feedback was mixed, with appeals to 'give it some time.' I have always believed that my purpose in this lifetime is to be a helper. Now, I was questioning that belief.

My partner and I went to dinner with her parents one evening. It was our favorite Chinese restaurant and the hope was that the dinner would take our minds off our loss, if not for just a brief period of time. Toward the end of the evening the waitress brought the fortune cookies to the table. My partner's father loved this part of a Chinese meal and the ritual was for everyone around the table to share their fortune. I usually humored him, but this evening I really wasn't in the mood for 'fun.' I was encouraged to participate, and rather reluctantly was the last to crack open a cookie. The fortune read: "Depart not from the path which fate has you assigned." Again, I felt the hair stand on the back of my neck, and chills ran up and down my spine. It was as if my Spirit Guide had put a pause on this process of life to send me a bulletin. Even the vernacular was in the language of my Spirit Guides. I mean, really, when was the last time you read a fortune cookie that started out with "Depart not"? Clearly, I was not to part from my blueprint. The fortune said "depart not." It did not say: "maybe," or "think about it," or "maybe you want to consider." It said "DEPART NOT." It was one of those moments where I feel like a Higher Power is hitting me over the head with reality, because I haven't been listening to more subtle messages. I heard. I listened. I did not depart. Instead, I continued to grieve throughout the coming weeks and months. My purpose is clear to me. That doesn't mean that I am not at risk, or that I won't experience tragedy along the way. It is a reminder to stay in the now, to be grateful for the gifts along the way, and to learn from the lessons that life has to teach.

# CHAPTER SIX

# SPIRIT GUIDES AND ANGELS

When I was a child I learned about angels through the Catholic Church. My understanding was that angels were in heaven and watched over "us." Because angels were a part of heaven, they seemed very far removed from my world. My perception was that "they" were "there" and I was too insignificant to be of their concern. As I grew older I began to question whether angels were a reality or a part of man's history that evidenced wishful thinking or over-imagination. I mean, really, the thought that angels were a reality appeared to be a product of fantasy.

My path in life was filled with the painful challenges that come with family dysfunction, mental illness and alcoholism. I was trapped in a dark world that was closing in on me. Despite years of sobriety and therapy the best I could do was function, and minimally at that. I entered into a very despairing time during my late twenties. It is not uncommon in therapy for things to get worse before they get better. I was definitely in the "things get worse" part of my treatment. I was too unstable to work in my field and I was finding it a challenge just to manage daily living skills. Despite being on medication I was so depressed it was a daily struggle to find the will to live. I was also extremely dissociative, and as a result I was rarely fully present mentally, emotionally, or spiritually.

It was during these years of desperation that I began to practice deep breathing and meditative states. Sometimes I would do this through new age music, sometimes through silent meditation, sometimes through writing (I could write for hours on end tapping into another form of consciousness) and sometimes through contemplative walking along the beach. One night I made an emergency call to my therapist. I was in a dissociative state, and in the course of our conversation a spirit from the other side introduced herself to my therapist. This spirit was named "Shannon" and she announced herself as being "of the light." At the time my therapist believed that this was a Spirit Guide. Until that point, I had never heard the term "Spirit Guide." My therapist explained that Spirit Guides were on the "other side" (what I used to refer to as heaven) and that they were available to assist us on this earthly plane. Essentially, Spirit Guides are our own private mentor or guide. They volunteer for the task, in order to assist us, themselves, and ultimately God in evolving. They are full of knowledge and wisdom, and love. Sylvia Browne does a much better job explaining about Spirit Guides, and I'd recommend any of her books to further your knowledge on the subject.

My knowledge about Spirit Guides and Angels came first through experience, then through self-education via reading. Shannon was definitely not a part of my personality. In other words, she was not a part of who I am. She was from the Other Side, and was a quiet presence. That time on the phone with my therapist was the only time that Shannon spoke to either me or her. She just needed to let us know that she existed. She communicates her presence through a loving white light. I have come to believe that she is an Angel, and not a Spirit Guide, as she does not readily interact with me. However, knowing about her opened my mind to Beings on the Other Side. Once I became open-minded to the possibility that there was an open line of communication available to me from the Other Side, it opened the door for my Spirit Guides to emerge.

Hanna was the first to introduce herself, coming to me through my journaling. While journaling I must have entered a meditative state, enabling Hanna to channel through my writing. I knew that it was not I that was writing, as the style and vocabulary was not mine. Her grammar and vocabulary was from another century and very formal. She was very quiet and shy, yet had a bantering sense of humor that would put me in my place faster than I could quip back. Hanna had a calming presence that was very reassuring to me. It was not long before I had a visual of her. She had dark skin, long brown hair and frequently wore a hooded linen robe. I've never really had a visual of her face. I think that is because she is so shy. However, I don't need to see her face because when I feel her presence her personality gives me more identity than facial features would. It is evidence to me that the flesh is but a package, and really has nothing to do with the spirit within. Identity comes through spirit form, not physical form. Hanna routinely spoke to me during long walks on the beach. She was my spiritual teacher. I would walk along the beach, collecting shells, and I would ask questions. Hanna would then begin to lecture in a very patient loving tone. She would tell me truths about the laws of life, which were not only comforting to me but very helpful because it told me that there is Purpose and Order to things. Sometimes she speaks in riddles. For many years I have heard her say: "There are three things I want you to remember." That's all she would say. I would be like: "Ok. What are they?" She'd never answer. She'd just keep repeating: "There are three things I want you to remember." She must really want me to remember because the suspense of finding out the answer is killing me. Actually, I've decided not to play this little game anymore, and I'm just waiting for her to decide when she wants to advise me. We are in a stalemate on this one because neither one of us is budging. I'm not asking, and she's not telling.

Hanna and I spent many months in this mentoring relationship before a second Spirit Guide came forward. Tron also came forward while I was journaling. Tron is a very strong male, who was a warrior. My best guess to place him in history would be during ancient Greece or the Roman Empire. My first image of Tron was a visual of him dressed in his breast plate of armor and helmet. He is very handsome, muscular, with a chiseled face. He is also full of pride and honor. Tron is most certainly not as patient as Hanna. He feels more like my spiritual body guard. My belief is that Tron and I were warriors fighting side by side in battle in another life time. He feels like my blood brother. There is a very tight bond that is glued with honor and love. He is a mentor to me and has a protective watch over me. Hanna is more inclined to 'yield to the resistance' whereas Tron will assert himself with conviction. Both have remained with me for well over fifteen years now. They are a constant source of wisdom and guidance, readily available if I appeal to them. They can both be very frustrating, humorous, stubborn, and wise. Always, they communicate abundant love.

The influence that Shannon, Hanna, and Tron had on my life was profound. So profound, that I decided to legally change my name. I adopted Shannon as my last name. When I sign my name the "S" from Shannon's name swoops around me in a representation of her white light surrounding me. I changed my middle name to "H" to represent Hanna. I didn't legally take the name Hanna because Vickie Hanna Shannon sounded too much like "Rosanne Rosanna Danna". So, Vickie H. Shannon will have to suffice. As for Tron, well I couldn't see extending my name to four names. Tron and I conferred on this and decided that he is so close to me he doesn't need to be represented in my name. Tron would say: "I am by your side; I need not be a part of your name."

What follows are journal entries where Tron and Hanna have channeled through me. I share them with you because they had a message that they would like others to hear. In fact, this book is a reality only because of the persistent prompting that I received from Tron and Hanna. They kept telling me to write. It is my hope that you will hear their profound wisdom and appreciate them as much as I.

The following entries are excerpts of conversations that occurred while journaling at my computer. For clarity and simplicity I have used italics when I have dictated from Hanna or Tron.

## Tron
### *Spiritual Awakenings*

It was late afternoon on January 31, 1992. I had been profoundly depressed all that week, and particularly that day. Suicide was no longer an "option" for me, yet the depression was so profound that I found myself wanting to die. I needed an escape, some relief, from the waves of despair that kept washing over me. I decided to take a nap before preparing dinner, as this coping mechanism frequently assisted me in preventing myself from doing something self-destructive. I was sleeping long enough to have been dreaming, because my "dream-in-progress" was suddenly interrupted.

A male spirit appeared before me. He was in white. I am not a holy roller by any stretch of the imagination, nor am I religious, but I would have to say that his presence felt as I would imagine feeling in the presence of Jesus. I am not saying it was Jesus, because he did not address himself as such. It may have been my Spirit Guide "Tron," or an angel. Regardless of who it was (as it appears unimportant) the experience I was to have was, indeed, a powerful one. The spirit knew of my internal turmoil, and stated very quietly and matter-of-factly: *"Reach in, let go and relax."* I listened but was at a loss, as I did not know how to "reach in." He repeated his statement for me, only this time he appeared to be guiding me throughout his instruction. *"Reach in* (pause) *let go* (pause) *and relax* (pause)." His words were the same and yet he was projecting a feeling of encouragement to me. It was as if he was trying to show me how, through a physical sensation. By now I had realized how to 'reach in.' The process was so simple once I understood the pathway to my pain. In fact, I felt an open channel to the source of my despair. Yet the rest of his instruction seemed more difficult than the words would suggest. I had 'reached in' alright, but I was gripping my pain in desperation.

*"Let go* (pause) *and relax,"* he stated. He spoke with patience and yet I felt an almost urgent push from Him. I couldn't manage to let go. It was too frightening. I was holding on with all my might.

*"Let go,"* he stated. With that there was an image of a green cross. It started out small, and grew larger. Then it started pulsing and turning white, until it exploded into a burst of White Light. I let go instantly. *"And relax,"* he stated. What immediately followed was a deep state of relaxation. I want to describe this state as the same thing that happens when one breathes one's last breath and the body sighs in deliverance, acknowledging a passage of life from one form to another. And yet, I wonder why I would even say such a thing, as I have not "crossed over" to the other side. Actually, I was in somewhat of an altered state. I was conscious on different levels. I knew that I was sleeping, and yet I was also aware of everything going on around me. I even heard a large sigh come forth from my body, and then felt all my muscles relax. My whole body sank further into my bed. I was more relaxed than I had ever experienced. I wasn't floating, and I wasn't out of my body. I was conscious of separation of body and spirit, and I was present

in both at the same time. It was as though I had been given a glimpse of transcendent peace.

My male spirit was gone. He left as quickly as he had appeared. From my description, the experience appears to have taken much time. Yet, it was very brief. He taught me how to reach in and let go, and stayed with me until I was fully relaxed. This was not a dream. I know the difference. It was an incredibly empowering experience. It was a gift, and I am very grateful for the privilege of having experienced it.

I am not dead yet, because I know I am not supposed to be. It's as though God provides some relief, a reminder, and encouragement to continue when I am ready to give up. It's as though He is saying to me: *"Child, I am with you. You are not alone. Take this and rejoice in it, and teach others as I am teaching you. You have much to do, and your time has not come to be with me. Hold within you the knowledge that I am with you, and carry on."*

## The Soul (By Tron)

*Individuals are at their busy lives, solely focused on the experience at hand, and almost forgetful or unconscious of the soul that stirs within. So many humans, it seems to me, are not in touch with their souls but the thing is the soul is there. The soul remains there, unless evil forces it out. Then just the body is there, and the machine functions, and the person walks and talks and does…without a Conscious or Guiding Purpose for* <u>what</u> *it does. And without a Conscious or Guiding Purpose for what it does, there becomes an avenue for behavior which is dictated by other sources of darkness and evil. Those who would seek evil may eventually repent and become aware of the Guiding Purpose in their lives…the soul and body may become aligned. Yet, there is a point at which the individual so fervidly bent on evil cannot return to the Source of Light—**not** because God would not make it so, but because those deeds that were done prevent such an individual from finding himself or herself. It is as though the soul once forced out, finds a new purpose. When body and soul are denied harmony through voluntary persistent evil, a discord is forever created. And so, there will always be darkness and evil. Evil perpetuates darkness. Goodness assures us of continued Light. Goodness, God, Love…all mean Light.*

*So, there are those who would cast aside their souls, those who are only semi-conscious…and thus "lost" (actually not lost, but distracted), and those who have* a conscious awareness of their Guiding Purpose in this life. Do not be fooled by the term "conscious awareness", for this does not mean that these individuals know all, or are superior in some form or another. They are not looked upon as any more beautiful, or any more loved. To be truly conscious, one would know this without thought or deliberation. The conscious (those who have an awareness of their soul, their spirit) are present as teachers—to teach in many forms and many ways and many things…but above all to teach love. In this way they are healers. The true healer does not heal from without, but facilitates another to heal from within… always mindful and respectful of that individual's own guiding force.

We are here to set one another free, to enjoy the earth, and to know the Light. A complicated procedure, with many twisting turns and tumultuous paths…yet always the promise of eternal light if one is free to…reach in …let go…and relax.

-2/20/92

## _Educate yourself._ (By Tron)

In order to educate yourself you must be willing to open your mind to new thoughts and ideas. Gather information by reading, listening to others, listening to yourself, talking with others. Question what you learn, no matter who it comes from. Beware of so-called "authorities." Question, think, and then listen inside to find if you can use the information to grow. If there is something you absolutely positively cannot relate to –look again for it probably applies. Denial is a crippling blindness.

Sometimes the most important lessons come from those who seemingly have nothing to offer. If what you hear or see produces a sense of resistance within you (your gut tightens), then honor the resistance. Put it aside and come back to it another time—either you are not ready to hear the information, or the information is laden with beliefs or messages that do not promote growth.

Education produces awareness.

When one is aware, one has choices. When one has choices, one is free to grow. When one is free to grow, there is an open path for a positive force of energy to enter one's life. With that energy comes healing, and with healing, recovery, and with recovery, a renewed life.

*The process is more important than attaining the goal, for without the process the goal is unattainable. If you remember nothing else, remember this: If you ask with honesty and a willingness to hear the answer, the answer will always come. Learn to listen for the answer from within, for you hold the key which unlocks the door. By searching for a power greater than yourself, you will find It has been inside you all the while.*

## Hanna
### *Surrender*
OK, Hanna, you appear to be willing to speak.

*No, child, you appear willing to listen.*

Point noted. So far, if I have heard you correctly, you come from a warm place; you lived in a village in a mountainous area. I knew all that already. What I didn't know was that you had brown skin. Why do you tell me about your people?

*So that you will know of yourself.*

You aren't a part of me are you?

*I am with you. I speak through you. I share a connection. I am for and about you. Is that not a "part" of you?*

That doesn't answer my question. Did I make you up, or are you from another life or something?

*Life is continuous, child. It flows as one. How is it that I come from "another life," when time has never stood still?*

You know what I mean. Why can't you just answer me straight? Why does everything have to be shrouded in mystery and bits and pieces? Forget it, don't answer that. I heard you say that I am your child. Is everyone your child?

*All are my children, yet all are not mine to look after.*

So what is it that you supposedly have to say to me? I don't get it. This process takes too long.

*Be patient, dear child, your answers will come.*

Who is Tron, Hanna, and what does 3001 mean? I know, I know, I know…I ask too many questions. It's quiet all of a sudden, so I guess you went away again. Hello? Hanna? Request: If you do have something to tell me, will you please tell me. I'm afraid to hear it, but I have to get over these fears because they stand in the way of my getting better. Look, I really want to do this, and I'm beginning to think that I can't do it unless I <u>fully trust</u> you and my therapist—a spirit and a human.

*This healing cannot take place unless both are complete. You are very near total trust in your therapist, but my intangibility makes it more difficult for you to find total trust in me. Complete your trust in your therapist, so that you may believe in the power of woman-spirit. It is then that you will be able to believe and understand in the power that I offer, with open arms, to you. You must do this. You must place your life in our hands, without reserve, or you will not have the ability to endure the battle. Sometimes you must completely surrender, despite well-established fears. With such surrender comes faith, and with faith a path to attain that which is rightfully yours. Trust is the foundation, upon which you will build faith, hope, security, and a true meaning for that which you call love. Listen to your therapist when she tells you it is yours to behold. The price of surrender is no longer what you were once taught. It is time, child, for you to learn the lesson as it was Originally intended. Conquer your fear, and you will conquer the darkness that beckons. You are more powerful than darkness if you conquer your fear. That is the bridge between darkness and eternal light. We are here to guide you. We have waited with you for this time. It has come. Go back to your therapist and work on surrender, and do not hold back. You will only receive that which you give.*

-1/14/92

## Trusting

Hanna? I know you can hear me. I hear nothing in return. Is it me? Do I open a channel half way? I am so self-willed. I know that it is my own fear that blocks you out. Yet, I do hear you at times. Please, keep trying to get through to me. I realize that I will have to do my part. That it takes effort on my part for me to be receptive. How silly it is that effort is defined in this case as 'being open'. Open to what? Why is that so hard? Am I really that lazy? If it is truly fear, what am I afraid of? I know you do me no harm. I know that you, and the others, are here to assist me, to guide me, to comfort me. Is it not my purpose on this plane to have a conscious contact with you? I feel like I'm entering a time in this life where I am traversing into the unknown. Yet, I feel like I am going more willingly. I really don't need the pseudo-control that I believed existed. Despite my best efforts, I continue to get in the way. I block myself of growth, yet I grow just the same…albeit slower. I want to say that I am ready to give myself, my will over. I know I still have choices; it's just that somewhere along the way I took back the reins and decided that I was in charge—to the point that I didn't need any input. As if I know what's best for me. I cringe at the thought.

So…what are you here to teach me? What is this new lesson all about? You've obviously got my attention. You must delight in the response I have been having. I've been caught off guard once again. Somehow, I think it may be better that way in the sense that I know this is not something that I orchestrated. It is coming from outside me, without any of my influence. I hope to stay open, consciously open, in a similar fashion. I don't know what this is all about, but I am willing to be a part of this process. I want to be more conscious. Somehow one must be able to experience on a spiritual as well as human level. If that is possible, that is what I would like--to be connected to the process, looking for (being open to the lesson) whatever that may be, within that process. Letting go of the fear.

*What do you have to lose? What do you have to gain? Wherein lay the trouble within your heart? Do you not know that we would not lead you astray? You continue to wrestle with the process, this process. Stop 'thinking' about what is 'right' as this is only an attempt to control. Have you not learned from the past? Do you truly believe that you are here for perfection? There is nothing to 'do right' here, child. Be a part of the process, and you are 'being right.' There is much to do, much to learn. It is important that you learn with an open heart, and to leave the mind to censor elsewhere. You are about to learn trust. Trust of a different kind. Trust the lesson. Trust with an open heart. You are capable of trust, for you learned that with your therapist.*

Was it trust or love that I learned with my therapist?

*Both. This is a new trust, a new love that you have yet to learn. Love takes many forms. Love is a universal term with many layers.*

I am learning layers.

*Yes.*

Must I learn love on a human level to fully feel it on a spiritual level? I thought I had it the other way around. I know spiritual love.

*You only begin to know.*

OK, but you know what I mean. How does learning on a human level help me?

*It is a slowing of the process that brings deeper meaning, knowing, on a spiritual level. You will 'know' with every fiber.*

I hear you and I want to believe, but the skepticism remains.

*Believe anyway.*

So, I am to proceed. I see your hand, Hanna. Can I grasp it?

*It is extended for you to grasp. You are not alone.*

You are truly patient. Take me and lead me through this process. Please talk to me.

*Please listen.*

## The Ides of March, 1992

Tron, Shannon, Hanna? Are you there? I need your wisdom. I need your input. I feel caught between two worlds today. I need to have more contact with you. I need a better understanding of this psychic part of me. I need to be able to distinguish between what is mine, and what is projected from another's soul. Teach me how to communicate with other souls. Teach me how to reach them so that I can quell their fear, so that they may heal themselves. I realize in asking such, I ask for you to teach me to do so for myself, first.

Help me to develop my abilities so that I am open—open to listen to what you and perhaps other guides have to say to me. I am an instrument through which you may speak and teach. I am willing, and want to learn. The door is not fully open, and never has been. Is that because of my trauma? Will I have access to the spiritual world in which you are, once I am healed? My purpose on this earth is many things, and yet I have always believed in my heart that one purpose is to be able to be present here, yet present (or conscious) of the spiritual world as well. I know this because I can be psychic while awake, as well as asleep. I believe that I have this ability for a reason, and that I haven't even begun to tap into it. I believe that I am to use this ability to reach many people.

I am here to reach others, am I not? I am here to comfort and heal the soul, am I not? You must know my purpose even more than I. Must it be a mystery? You teach me all the time. I am learning about the lessons that I have to accomplish. Who is naming these lessons for me? It's like I can feel you taking me by the hand and showing me what I have learned and what my next task is.

There was the lesson of love. It was powerful, and yet it is not complete, is it? Love is multi-dimensional. I have just begun. I still have one more thing, regarding love, to learn with my therapist. It is a lesson we must both learn together. I hear you. I do not understand what else I could possibly learn, but I hear you.

There is the lesson of faith. I am stubborn. It will be hard to teach me faith. It is so very frightening. Yes, I realize that overcoming my own fear will be the key for me, but it is like asking me not to breathe anymore and assuring me that I will not die in the process.

There is the lesson of hope—one that appears to be a very gradual unfolding. Sometimes I am full of hope, and then it vanishes as though it was never really there at all. It has always been that way. That is why I cannot trust hope—Yes, I know that. It is also crucial if I am ever to know true happiness, true joy.

## *Tron:*

*In order to be free to experience joy, there must be hope because hope is the essence of positive, the essence of safety. You cannot feel joy unless you feel hope, and you cannot feel hope unless you know safety, because safety assures one that goodness will prevail. Hope is like waiting for goodness to return, whether it be for five minutes or an eternity.*

*There is the lesson of trust, which you have not completely mastered yet. Your fear prevents you from experiencing trust to its fullest potential. How can you expect to facilitate others, if you cannot fully trust? Your time will come, as it is meant to be, but it is not yet. Do not set time constraints upon yourself, as you will not fully benefit from the lessons you must learn. Learn now, so that you may spend the rest of your time freeing others. Then they will be your greatest teachers.*

*Fear is your greatest obstacle. You must learn to overcome it. Fear is not to be conquered. You miss the point entirely. Reach in, let go, and relax. Do you not remember? We are not here to catch your fall, as there is nothing that you are falling from. You will not "go anywhere" if you let go. Where do you think you will go if you release your fears?*

I will be hurt if I let go of my fears. I will be injured. If I fully trust, and hope, and—

*Tron: And what? Love? You did fully love and you were not harmed.*

But, Tron, trust and hope are different. And so is giving up fear. Fear protects me.

*Tron: It also isolates you.*

But isn't it better to be protected even at the cost of isolation? Haven't I been hurt enough?

*Tron: Are you satisfied in your isolation? Does that cause you no injury? Was it not you who moments ago asked for an open channel?*

But I have nothing to fear from a spiritual world. I know that world better than I know this one.

(Pause)

*Hanna:*
*You also know that to be fully open you will have to be open to other's pain. We have pain, child. Do you not know that? It is not the pain you are accustomed to, but we have our own familiarity with pain. Do you not remember my tears?*

Hanna! It's you. Yes, I do remember.

*Hanna: We feel, with a certain detachment, but we do feel. When you ask for an open channel you also ask to receive without condition, any information which is doth provided. If you are not in harmony with fear, if you cannot learn to work with it, you will succeed in cloaking yourself in this "protective" isolation. Suicide is the ultimate in protective isolation. Suicide is the validation of one's inability to let go of fear. It is a sad time for us, as it represents a soul that was unable to be reached. It is important for you to be reached in your world. Do you not understand this?*

I only understand that it is a lesson for me- that unless I learn love, trust, hope, faith, security, and to be at peace with fear, I will not know peace in this world. I will not know Goodness in this world. The point is not to find Light in the spiritual world, because I know that it exists there. The point is to be able to experience it on earth. I have to regain what was taken away from me.

*Hanna: No, child, you were misled. They could not take your Light away from you. That was an illusion. You need not take back anything. What you need is to reject the fear that they placed upon you. That was not inherently yours. Love, Light, Trust, Faith, Hope…these things are inherently yours.*

Oh, Hanna, you make it seem so simple, when it is not.

*Hanna: If you make it complicated it will be.*

I wish I had the ability to come back at you as quickly as you come back at me. I cannot compete with you.

*Hanna: Yet you will not cease in trying.*

Are you done? I mean, is there anything more that I am to know this evening? Are there lessons that I missed? What do I do now? Should I be <u>doing</u> something? What comes first—hope, trust, faith, love? How does this work? Is there an order to this? Does it all depend on my ability to reject fear?

*Hanna: You don't reject fear.*

But, you just told me to reject the fear they put upon me.

*Hanna: Reject the idea that it was inherently yours. Learn to acknowledge what is yours, and what was projected onto you. Differentiate the two. Take what is yours and embrace it. In so doing, you will find peace.*

But, what do you mean "embrace"? That's just a fancy word to me. I cannot feel that word. How can I embrace fear when I want to repel it into another galaxy? Do I have to learn this? Can't we just forget about the fear part?

*Hanna: Yes, and you can also forget about the love and hope and…*

I know. Shit. Can't you humor me once in a while?

*Hanna: I am not here for humor. You are not yet ready to embrace fear. There are other tasks before you. Continue in your work with your therapist. We are here to guide. We are present. Yet, do not forget, child, that it is your task to accomplish. The answers are within you, and they will evolve with time. Do not rush process. Process has nothing to do with time. Time is a marker. It is continual. It is a measure. Process is eternal in that it is life. Time is not life. Measure time, but do not measure process. Process knows no time. Your process is unfolding. In time you will reap the harvest of the seeds in which you have sowed. Be patient. The yield will be plentiful.*

# CHAPTER 7

# MEDITATE ON THIS

Meditation is somewhat of an enigma. There are different styles, both formal and informal. There are individuals who consider themselves experts on the subject, each with a different format that is somehow the "correct" way to meditate. There are others who claim they know nothing about meditation, yet practice it daily. It is a time-honored practice, dating back over thousands of years, yet recently (within the past fifty years) it seems to be undergoing a comeback. Meditation is considered to be the path to enlightenment in many eastern traditions. Yet it is not just reserved for eastern faiths, but a suggested practice of many religions. It is also incorporated into the eleventh step of Alcoholics Anonymous. While it may be somewhat of a conundrum, it is also undeniably a historically diligent and revered practice of the human race. It seems to me that anything that can exist throughout history, regardless of race, religion, age, status, or gender must be Divine in nature. There simply must be a good reason why the practice of meditation exists. Whether it is for the goal of enlightenment, alleviation of stress, lowered blood pressure, self-discipline, or a desire to connect with God, meditation has its benefits.

Over the years, regardless of how I have practiced meditation, I have often wondered if I was "doing it" right. Sometimes I have noticed that I felt relaxed, at peace, and centered after meditating. Other times I have finished a meditation feeling frustrated due to the fact that my mind was continually racing from thought to thought. I've even fallen asleep while meditating, which seems to automatically disqualify me from the "doing it" right category. Regardless of my perceived success or failure, I have been meditating on and off for over twenty-five years. In all that time, I can honestly say that I have only had one incredibly profound experience. In fact, it was so liberating for me that it was worth all those other times that it felt like "nothing" happened.

I had been attending a weekly meditation group for approximately six months. The facilitator utilized a combination of relaxation techniques and guided imagery. I usually felt deeply relaxed and at peace after these evening meditations. We had been meeting in the chapel of a church, which was a very peaceful setting and which also provided comfortable chairs. Due to unfortunate circumstances, we had to move the meditation to a small group room at my office. The chairs were not as comfortable, and on this particular evening I was sitting in a small wood chair, that had a wicker seat. The facilitator began as usual, with progressive relaxation. At some point the sound of her voice drifted off. From this point on it is very difficult for me to describe what happened, as there are no words to adequately describe my experience. In fact, the felt sense of this experience defies the ordinary five senses that we have to depict an event.

I'll begin by saying that I had a conscious awareness of nothingness. I was suddenly aware that I was in blackness. This blackness had no negative connotations. It also had no positive connotations. It was just blackness. There was no sense of temperature. This blackness was not cold, nor hot. It was a completely neutral environment. It was just black space. I was in this space, yet not in my body.

If I were to walk outside with you at night, and point up into the sky, you would see stars amid a black backdrop. The black between the stars is where I was. I was just "up there," not floating, not hovering, not doing anything. I was just there, in total nothingness, with no feelings, no thoughts, and no sensation. There was no external or internal conflict. There was no worry. There was no stimulation. There was just this experience of black "nothing".

When I say I had a "conscious awareness of nothingness," that is not an accurate statement. The fact is, I wasn't even aware that I was experiencing this black nothingness until I heard this thought: "Where am I?" The thought seemed to echo. Then a second thought: "Am I sleeping?" Then an answer: "No, I'm in this uncomfortable chair." With that thought, I was back in my body again. The event was over, yet the significance of the experience continued to work through me for well over a day.

It wasn't until I processed this event that I was able to realize I had been in the blackness of the galaxy. Or, maybe I was in a place of infinity, or a black hole, or maybe just in a space between the stars. I don't have a mind set or previous experience to tell you exactly where I was, other than I was definitely "up there" amid the night sky.

All of that is significant enough, yet with further introspection I came upon something even more profound, an awakening of sorts. When I was in the black nothingness, it was as if I was in some sort of hibernated state. Almost as if I didn't even exist. Upon thinking this through, I realized that I must have existed. One does not cease to exist, and then return from nonexistence. I was there, yet there was no normal evidence of my presence. This was a kind of existence that I was at total peace with, yet seemingly not familiar with from the human perspective.

And then it hit me. It was my thought that gave me existence. Rene Descartes said "I think, therefore I am." My thought gave me a consciousness existence. Yet it wasn't as if I didn't exist prior to the thought. I was there, all right, but where was "there." "There" was this unfamiliar spiritual plane. I was so connected, so at peace, so at one with the All of the Universe. I was there, at one, with the great I AM. *There was no difference.* I and God were one and the same, in this blissful nothingness. It was my thought that gave me separation, an existence apart from God.

Isn't that the greatest gift that God could give us? God has granted us our own identity with the gift of conscious thought. With this gift of thought comes free will to make our own choices. The problem with such a gracious gift is that we don't know how to use that gift without engaging in acts of self-defeat. We engage in self-destructive acts on a personal, community, and global basis. The ego, or conscious thought, is what sets us apart. The consequence is this illusion that the small "i am" is somehow the great I AM. It's as if we somehow lost the translation and got it backwards. We are only one with the great I AM when we don't think. We are only one when we are connected. Our thoughts separate us. Our mind separates us. The very thing that so many of us revere is the very thing that separates us.

I am not my mind. I am not my body. The "I" in me is my spirit, and that part of me is always connected to Source. I am one with God. God is in me, through me, around me, with me. I am God and God is me, as long as I don't separate myself with thought. For that matter every sentient being is God and God is every sentient being. It's right there for all of us to be connected, yet we have to give up personal identity, personal agenda, to achieve it. I believe this is why there are so few who have achieved enlightenment. Detaching from one's thoughts is the greatest personal sacrifice that one can offer—a high price for Nirvana. Detaching from my own thoughts for a few minutes during a meditation is one thing. Detaching from my thoughts for a lifetime is another thing entirely. The experience assured me that I am not alone. It assured me that I can connect with Source, provided I detach from conscious thought.

This is all just an exercise, this thing called life. I began to see that I take this all way too seriously and most certainly too personally. I also began to feel love, real Grace, for my fellow brothers and sisters. I feel connected to everyone in a way I never imagined. No wonder psychic abilities exist—we are all one. If we as a human race could just get this concept on a global scale, the shift in human relations would be miraculous indeed. If we could just put aside our religious thoughts long enough to realize how to connect to Source, the barriers would melt like an ice cube on a hot metal roof. It is impossible not to shift when you realize the path to Source is through connection. I am wired, I am programmed to separate. My task is to recognize that despite my separateness, I am always connected as a spiritual being. It is my human experience that separates me. The human part, the "skin suit," is really just an illusion that reinforces my separateness. I can and will have a human experience. I have an opportunity to recognize my separateness and learn the lessons I am here to learn. It is my responsibility to make a conscious decision on a daily basis to connect to Source by detaching from thought- even if I'm just detaching from thought (from myself) from time to time. I guess "ET" would say "phone home." I "phone home" by connecting, by tapping into the nothingness of the One.

Meditate on that.

# AFTERWARD

Each time I wanted to give up on this book a friend, family member or Spirit Guide would encourage me to continue. My hope is that the content is thought provoking, heart-felt, entertaining, and educational. It takes frequent acts of courage and stamina to remain on the path of growth and transformation. I have healed through family dysfunction, alcoholism, and my own mental illness. I am here to say that healing is possible. Being at peace internally is possible. There is a path out of pain that is well worth the time and effort. *Stay on your path.* Read. Find support. Get help. Link up with others who are also on a path of personal growth and transcendence. *Trust the process.* Get in touch with the spiritual being that is you. There is a reason for all of this, whether you recognize it or not. Remember: Reach in, let go, and relax. And don't forget to breathe. Recognize that the human experience is about the lessons that will transcend you to a higher level of being. Embrace the lessons.

# ABOUT THE AUTHOR

*Vickie H. Shannon* is a Licensed Mental Health Counselor and a Certified Addictions Professional in Florida. Vickie obtained her Bachelor of Science in Education (BSE) in 1985 from the State University of New York College @ Cortland. In 2001, Vickie received her Master of Education (M.Ed.) in Mental Health Counseling from Florida Atlantic University. She has approximately twenty five years experience in the field of addiction, and specializes in co-occurring mental health disorders. Vickie is currently in private practice in Vero Beach, Florida. She is also one of a trio of women who provide educational lectures and workshops through Vero Quest. For more information about Vero Quest go to the website at www.myveroquest.com